GET STARTED IN CREATIVE WRITING

Stephen May

With additional material by Jodie Draber

Get Started in Creative Writing

Stephen May

With additional material
by Jodie Daber

First published in Great Britain in 2008 by Hodder & Stoughton. An Hachette UK company.

First published in US in 2008 by The McGraw-Hill Companies, Inc.

This revised edition published 2014.

British Library Cataloguing in Publication Data: a catalogue record for this title is available from the British Library.

Library of Congress Catalog Card Number: on file.

10 9 8 7 6 5 4 3 2 1

Typeset by Cenveo® Publisher Services.

Printed and bound in Great Britain by CPI Group (UK) Ltd, Croydon CR0 4YY.

Hodder & Stoughton policy is to use papers that are natural, renewable and recyclable products and made from wood grown in sustainable forests. The logging and manufacturing processes are expected to conform to the environmental regulations of the country of origin.

Hodder & Stoughton Ltd

338 Euston Road

London NW1 3BH

www.hodder.co.uk

Acknowledgements

The author and publisher are grateful to the following writers for their contributions to this book:

David Armstrong, Anthony Clavane, Christopher George, Camilla Hornby, Mark Illis, Jenny Lecoat, Ian Marchant, Jacob Polley, Monique Roffey, Willy Russell, Caroline Smailes, Jo Verity and Lee Weatherly.

Contents

About the authors

Stephen May is an award-winning novelist, playwright and TV writer. His most recent novel, *Life, Death, Prizes!* (Bloomsbury), was published in 2012. He runs popular writing workshops throughout the UK. www.sdmay.com

Jodie Daber received her Master's degree in Creative Writing from the University of Huddersfield. She has published several short stories and is working on her first novel.

Introduction

The fact you are reading this book suggests that you are serious about your writing. The fact that you are taking the time to read a guide to writing rather than just leaping in to begin your novel or short-story collection suggests that you are not a brash type, overburdened with self-belief and confidence. The opposite is probably true. You already doubt yourself, wondering whether you really have anything original to say or any way properly to express it. This self-doubt is one major reason you have put off doing anything with your writing until now. I know this; I've felt this too. We would-be writers all have.

This feeling that you might not have any actual talent is one you share with nearly every writer, however successful they are. It's one of the things that mark you out as a writer: writers are quite horribly insecure, always unwilling to believe that they have written something worthwhile and at the same time touchy about criticism. Writing is a kind of emotional bungee jumping: it's terrifying and exhilarating all at the same time.

But you have already taken an important step on the road to becoming the very best writer you can be. You have decided to enlist some help.

Some of your friends have probably tried to put you off reading a book like this (assuming that any of your friends know that you want to write – so many new writers keep it a secret, not wanting to be thought weird or that they are somehow 'getting above themselves'). 'You can't teach writing,' they say. 'Writers are born, not made.' There is some truth in that. The urge to write, and the determination to keep at it in spite of all the distractions that life puts in the way, has to be dredged from somewhere within you and no one can teach that – though it gets easier with practice. The desire to improve is probably innate, too. And you have already proved you have got that desire because you have bought or borrowed this book.

Get Started in Creative Writing is intended to give you a chance to attempt all the major forms of prose writing, and to provide you with the information you need to do this in an enjoyable way. Whether you decide that you are a short-story writer, a novelist, a children's writer, a playwright, a screenwriter, a journalist, a blogger or any combination of these, then I hope this book will provide a useful and enjoyable companion. Whether you see writing as a hobby, as a way of passing on your memories or as a way of earning a living in the future, *Get Started in Creative Writing* should give you the building blocks you need. And I am always interested in hearing from new writers, so feel free to get in touch via my website www.sdmay.com with your feedback or your own stories of your writing life.

An earlier Teach Yourself book on creative writing was written over ten years ago by the novelist and poet Dianne Doubtfire, and I am indebted to her for her groundwork, just as I am indebted to her former student Ian Burton, who picked up the baton for its subsequent editions. Some of their exercises remain. And of course I'd like to thank all the writers and students who helped provide material. Some did this directly, in the form of exercises, and others helped through informal conversations about writing, which were then transmuted into the substance of this book.

How to use this book

This book is designed to save you time. It's a guide to the short cuts that you might miss if you were travelling what can be a lonely road entirely on your own.

Get Started in Creative Writing is not a literary sat nav. It can't guide you to publication, fame and fortune in easy, mechanically voiced steps. There's nothing in this book that you couldn't find out for yourself, but it might take you years of painful trial and error with many discouraging knock-backs along the way. You'll get some of those anyway – discouraging setbacks are part of the process of becoming a fully realized human being, never mind becoming a writer – but this book will, I hope, mean that you skirt around the more obvious pitfalls, while honing a style that is uniquely yours.

What I have tried to do in *Get Started in Creative Writing* is distil some of the best advice from writers who have between them spent many, many thousands of hours thinking about, talking about, and teaching writing. I have drawn on the practical guidance of hundreds of writers – some of the best in the contemporary writing world – in all genres and at all stages in their writing career. Some of them have offered exercises that can be used to develop your skills and confidence; others have given me practical ways to generate ideas and professional tips.

I have also, of course, drawn on my own background and practice as a struggling writer as well as my time as a teacher. The book includes many exercises of my own which have sprung from my thinking about what might help a new writer who is unsure of the direction in which their writing may take them. And you can be sure that everything I have written is from the heart and tested by experience.

Icons

Here's your key to the different types of exercise and features in the book:

Write – exercises where you'll be asked to create your own piece of writing

Snapshot – shorter exercises or some questions to help you consider a particular aspect of creative writing

Workshop – a series of guided questions that will help you reflect on a piece of writing – see below for a more detailed explanation

Edit – a chance to rework and strengthen a piece you've already created

Key quote – words of wisdom from those who know

Key idea – an important concept to grasp

Focus point – advice to take forward

Next step – where we're going next.

It is not necessary to do every exercise in order to benefit from this book. Nor is it necessary to do them in sequence. Equally, you might want to do those exercises you personally find particularly useful several times. Some might become part of your daily practice. I hope so. In fact, although I use the word 'exercise' throughout, you might prefer to think of them as 'games' or ways into writing.

THE WORKSHOP

This edition of *Get Started in Creative Writing* includes a brand-new exercise – the workshop. Creative writing workshops provide writers of all abilities and backgrounds with a space in which to share their work and get constructive feedback. They are also great places to meet like-minded people and share the agonies and ecstasies of becoming a writer. There's probably one happening near you. Ask at your local library or adult education centre for details. Some of them even have biscuits.

As a substitute for chatting to others in a real workshop about the writing you produce, this book includes a workshop exercise in each chapter. In these workshops you'll get the chance to review a piece of writing you created in an earlier exercise. There'll be a series of questions which should help you see your piece through new eyes, to identify what's successful and what isn't, and guide you towards ways to strengthen and hone your writing.

Writing is hard work, but it shouldn't feel like a slog. You should feel joy and pride, too. The exercises here are workouts that will help you put on writing muscle, but they are also fun. Many of them are suitable for more than one genre: for example, an exercise that works especially well for blossoming screenwriters may also work for playwrights and novelists. Be creative and feel free to plot your own path through this book.

Good luck!

Stephen May

1

Why write?

Forget what they say. Writing is easy. It is.

More or less every adult in this country can write. Most of us can fashion a sentence, however clumsily, and many people can use words very well. Think of all the people you know who are natural storytellers – people who can hold a group enthralled with a vivid account of something that happened to them, or who can get a room to explode in laughter with a quick one-liner. These people are known for their skill with words – their emails and texts are a joy to read because of the special colour they bring to their use of language, even with something quite dull – and yet none of them would consider themselves to be a writer.

Creative writing is also cheap, sociable and good for you. You don't need any special equipment but you do need to make time for your writing.

Creative writing is for everyone

Maybe you are one of those people who enjoys telling stories, or who gets a buzz from putting words in the right order; someone who delights in entertaining, informing and surprising friends, family and colleagues with words. Perhaps you enjoy writing even the dullest work communication: the famous Czech writer Franz Kafka had a day job as an insurance clerk but, by all accounts, his reports and minutes were always eagerly awaited by his colleagues because of their dry humour and elegant phrasing.

Unlike learning to play a musical instrument, writing does not demand hours and hours of repetitive practice every day. Neither does it demand expensive equipment. And unlike learning a foreign language, you don't need to go abroad or find someone else to practise with.

All you need to write is a pen, some paper and a place to go. And it doesn't need to be a particularly quiet or private place. You can write on the Tube, on the bus, in a café, during breaks at work, in bed. You can write during stolen moments at work, or after the kids have gone to bed. Writing in a car is perhaps not to be recommended, but even while driving there are ways of going about it. You can record your thoughts into a voice recorder or hands-free phone.

Creative writing is easy, natural, healthy, sociable, cheap and accessible. You don't need to be in perfect health or even physically fit. You don't have to have a degree or even a GCSE. You don't have to be young. You don't have to be good-looking. You don't have to be a certain age or a certain social class. Writing is completely democratic.

You just need to have something to say.

Why you want to write

Write down in one sentence of no more than 30 words why you want to write.

Tennessee Williams

'Why did I write? Because I found life unsatisfactory.'

Creative writing is natural

The philosopher Socrates said: 'The unexamined life is not worth living' and *his* words, as transcribed by Plato, have survived for several thousand years, so he knew what he was talking about. We live busy lives at a frantic pace. There often doesn't seem time just to 'stand and stare', as the poet W. H. Davies put it.

We spend so much of our time firefighting – reacting to events – that we leave ourselves little time to investigate the causes of all the small blazes in our lives. Why do we do the things we do? Why do we often feel hurt, neglected or sad? How can we be better parents, children, companions or lovers? How can we make sense of a world that contains 7 billion people? What is the point of it all?

Surely, at least, part of the point of life is to decide who we are and then to try to become that person? And how can we do that if we don't try to express our own unique way of seeing the world?

For some people their natural mode of self-expression will be one of the other arts. They will form a band or join a choir. They might take photographs or paint. Others will want to act or make films or create conceptual art. Still others will find that the extraordinary advances in digital technology will lead them down pathways to self-expression that didn't even exist ten years ago. But more and more of us, even in a digital world, want to use one of the oldest and simplest forms of self-expression. We want to tell stories. We want to tell our own stories or make up new ones. We want to transform our own existence into words that will delight, entertain, amuse or even horrify others.

The great English poet Ted Hughes believed that all these words had value. He believed that they all added to the 'sacred book of the tribe'. Our individual attempts to make sense of our lives contribute to the way humanity itself discovers its nature and purpose. In this sense, at least, everyone's story has equal value.

The beauty of the written word, as opposed to the spoken word in film and television, is that it invites you to linger. Film and television writing moves on at a faster pace, as the techniques and technology of editing develop. But a novel or short story allows the reader to choose the pace at which a story unfolds. We can immediately revisit passages that we especially like, take our time to unravel anything that we find obscure or difficult. But plays, films and television have their place in making sense of the world and we'll cover those art forms, too, later in this book.

Writing is good for you

Writing is a good way to reduce stress and relieve depression. Simply writing our troubles down can make them seem more manageable. Reliving past traumas on the page can reduce their power to haunt. Writing is way of taking control of your life. Therapy might not be your primary motivation for becoming a writer, but writing is certainly an effective way of keeping anxiety at bay and making you feel happier. If you write regularly, you will look and feel better without ever needing to get up from your chair! It is that powerful a magic.

Creative writing is sociable

This might seem an odd thing to say: the usual image of a writer is of someone solitary, a hermit. And it is true that in order to write successfully you need to have the ability and the discipline to shut yourself off in a room on your own. But writers also form a community and the more seriously we take our work the more important that community will be to us.

Of course, a lot of writers work with others anyway. Film and television writers are working with a whole army of collaborators, from the director to the stylist, from the producer to the gaffer's grip-boy (whatever that is!). Playwrights work even more closely with the directors and actors. But even for poets and novelists, the need for peer support can be incredibly important.

As you become more confident with your writing, you will probably want to join a local group of fellow writers. You will want to find supportive but candid friends who can act as first readers and trusted guides. You will also find personal benefits in providing this service for other people. You might want to attend intensive residential courses like those run by the Arvon Foundation or decide to undertake an MA in Creative Writing. But whatever paths writing leads you down, you are bound to meet like-minded people who are stimulating – sometimes infuriating – to be around. You will find more about the writing community in Chapter 16, 'Moving on'.

Finding a writing group

Using the library, the Internet or the local press, find out whether there are any writing groups nearby. Get their contact numbers and call them to see how they work and whether they would be suitable for you to join.

Creative writing is a family affair

Writing creatively is a good way to get and stay close to your family. Older family members may well have interesting stories and family secrets that can act as springboards for your own work. Your children and other younger relatives may want to know about the stories that you can tell. Very young children, of course, love stories – whether real or imaginary – and they are a very good and truthful audience.

If you are open about your writing, you might quickly find that it grows into a family project with people regularly asking you for bulletins on how the work is progressing. This can be good motivation for carrying on with it.

Listen to family stories

Ask someone in your extended family for a story that they haven't told you before. They don't have to be convinced that it is entirely true; it could be some kind of family legend from the distant past. Take notes and put them in a drawer to be worked on later.

Creative writing is cheap and accessible

In most fields of endeavour, it is unlikely that you would be able to get one-to-one tuition from the people at the top. If you wanted to be a top tennis pro, for example, even if you could afford it, how would you persuade someone like Andy Murray to give you a series of private lessons? He's a busy man! The same is also true of many areas of the arts. But in the field of creative writing your perfect mentors are always available. If you use your public library, your favourite authors are there, they are free, and they are present for as long as you need them. There is absolutely nothing to stop you spending weeks locked up alone with Tolstoy, or with Philip Roth, Sharon Olds, Sylvia Plath, Jackie Collins or Woody Allen.

Find inspiration in the work of others

Whoever your inspiration is, they are waiting for you. Dead or alive, mad or bad, the greatest writers are available as your guides. You don't have to rely on YouTube or on grainy footage of long-lost champions in order to study technique; you can bring their work home with you and focus on it in microscopic detail and in your own time. How-to books like this one are useful but by no means essential.

Read other writers

Make a short list of all the writers whose works you have found most inspiring. Now make sure that you fit in a trip to the public library when you next go shopping and take out some of their work. Reacquaint yourself with your heroes.

Next, try asking around among your friends, family and work colleagues for examples of writing that they have found particularly impressive. When you return your heroes to the library, make sure you replace them with some writing that has been recommended to you. Reading, more than anything else, is what will help you improve as a writer. Reading good work carefully is the fastest way to see visible developments in your own writing life. And it helps to have an open mind and a willingness to experiment in your reading tastes, too. Try not to be too dismissive of work you see being championed in the press or on television. On the other hand, reading something and then thinking, 'I could do better than that,' is a perfectly legitimate response. It can be inspiring to find a writer who has legions of admirers but who in your opinion is not actually such hot stuff. That's fine. I'd keep it to yourself for a little while, however!

Finding time to write

Everyone has time to write. It might be that something else will have to go (a favourite television show, staying late at the office, looking for eBay bargains, reading the paper – writers make sacrifices, there's no getting around this), but you'll find the time to write if you want to badly enough.

Suzanne Berne, the Orange prize-winning author of *A Crime in the Neighbourhood,* wrote her first book having been determined to set aside at least five minutes a day in which to write. If she achieved at least her daily five minutes, then she gave herself a little tick on the calendar. 'After a little while,' she says, 'I became obsessed with giving myself a tick every day. And if you can somehow manage a page a day, that's a novel in a year.'

 Focus point

If you write 1,000 words a day, that works out at a novel twice the length of *Great Expectations* every single year.

The double Carnegie-Medal-winning children's author Berlie Doherty would put a log on the fire after her children went to bed and write until the log burned out. Serious writers, those who make a success of it, will make time.

THE BEST TIME TO WRITE

Try writing at different times of day and in different locations to see what suits you. Do you work best in the evening, curled up on the sofa, or in the morning at the kitchen table? Perhaps you prefer to write in your lunch break in the local café? Some of us are night owls and some of us are morning people. Experiment until you find the time when your creative juices are at peak flow.

However much or little you write, regularity is the most important thing. Suzanne Berne's five minutes a day will achieve better results than a four-hour stretch every now and again. If you are really struggling to find time, try managing on seven hours' sleep instead of eight. If this doesn't work, then you have no choice: you have to get rid of the television. Nothing steals so much time in so insidious a manner as the television. You'll also save the cost of the licence fee in the UK and any digital or cable subscriptions, too. This means that writing will already be paying off for you.

THE SECOND-BEST TIME

There's a saying: 'The best time to plant a tree is 20 years ago. The second-best time is now.' Of course, you should really have got round to writing before this. But you can't do anything about that. There is no point in worrying about all the time that has past – it's what you write now and in the future that counts. Don't fret. Let it go.

Writing is one of those things that you can begin at any age. It doesn't require physical fitness, youth or even good health. Don't worry that some publishers seem to be like pop impresarios these days, always looking for a moody-looking teenager with a wild haircut and astonishing cheekbones; that some of them seem to regard their job as a branch of showbiz. We know otherwise and so do readers.

You have got to have lived a bit, and looked and listened a lot, before you have enough to say. Everything that has happened to you up to now is your material. The older you are, the more material you have to draw on. You are in a better position than someone just out of college. Wordsworth described writing as the setting down of 'emotion recollected in tranquillity' and said, 'Fill your paper with the breathings of your heart.' The more experience you have of life, the better you will be able to do this. You just need to make sure that you can find those moments of tranquillity!

A word about technology

You don't need a laptop to be a writer. And having one doesn't make you a writer either.

A light, simple-to-use laptop might be very useful, but it is by no means essential. The great Californian crime writer Peter Plate once found himself facing students upset that a temporary power failure meant that the computers weren't working in the building where he was conducting a writing class. His calm response made a powerful impression. He said, 'Don't confuse convenience with utility.' And with that he sent everyone off to write with a pencil.

Fewer people were interested in writing years ago and at least part of the reason was because it took a lot more physical effort to write using longhand or a typewriter. Writing was physical labour; words were almost literally wrenched from the writer. At any rate, writers were very much connected to their words in a physical way.

I am not suggesting that new writers should get rid of their PCs – for one thing the Internet can be an important market for a writer as well as a valuable research tool – but we should all be aware that just because our work looks professionally solid in its beautiful font, it doesn't mean that the writing itself is any good. The comfort that modern technology brings means that we have to be strict with ourselves.

Focus point

Work on a PC looks deceptively finished even at an early stage. Cut-and-paste facilities can trick you into believing that you are carrying out a serious edit when in fact you are merely moving inadequate material from one place to another.

Experiment with your kit

If you usually use a laptop, try writing by hand and vice versa. If you have a voice recorder on your phone, have a go at dictating to yourself. You may find that writing by hand slows you down and forces you to choose your words more carefully. On the other hand, writing on a computer can allow you to get your ideas down quickly and edit them with relative ease. Some people find that different methods suit different stages in the writing process, with note-making and plotting suiting paper and pen but the laptop coming into its own when it's time for a first draft. It's entirely up to you. Play around; experiment; find out what suits you.

Writing is easy because most people are educated enough to be able to put their thoughts down on paper. It is natural because to want to make sense of our loves and times is what makes us human. It is good for you because to seek to understand the world around us is to begin to change it. People who write live longer, more fulfilled lives that those who don't. This is because we are already turning our dreams into realities. Writing is sociable because writers gather in groups and classes in addition to working alone. We also collect stories from family members, workmates, passers-by and people in pubs, cafés and churches. We can't help getting involved in the lives of others, even if we work on the material we gather on our own.

The only reason not to write is if you simply want to get rich. You shouldn't write for the money because, generally speaking, there isn't any. Yes, we all know that J.K. Rowling, John Grisham, Dan Brown and a hundred others have got rich through writing, but that isn't *why* they do it. The money is a bonus. They'd do it anyway. They write because they have something to say. In fact, more than this, they write because they have a compulsion – an itch they have to scratch. You should write because, if you're a writer, you'll always be vaguely miserable (and a pain to be with) if you don't.

If that describes you, then you might as well just get on with it. But think hard about what it is you are trying to say. There are countless books, plays and scripts out there already. Why should anyone read yours? What have you got to say that adds to the huge canon of work already created?

Sometimes it will feel as if there are too many writers in the world and far too few readers. You can feel like a beggar endlessly sleeve-tugging at uninterested passers-by. You must somehow be able to entice readers to pick up your work and spend time with it alone, despite all the many competing pressures that might come from family, work, computer games or TV.

That can be hard. But if you work at your craft, and always remember that your stories have the same validity as anyone else's, you will be noticed. And, although a writer needs readers and these can be hard to find, you don't need very many. A few people genuinely looking forward to your next piece is all you need. Writers are unique among artists because of their symbiotic relationship with individual readers.

Of course, if you can't take criticism or rejection then writing isn't for you. All writers must face rejection; it's part of the job. It is much easier for editors and agents to say no than to say yes and take a huge risk on something that may not work. After all, another writer will be along in less than a minute. So don't be offended by people saying no to you. In fact, being ignored – being rejected – is good for your writing because it means you will learn to write smarter, to grab the attention and not let it go. You will develop guile and flair and stamina and, as the lightweights drop out, you will stand more chance of getting the audience you deserve.

Finally, find a voice that is uniquely yours. Stick to it. Grow with it. Tell the stories only you can tell and eventually doors will open.

Workshop

Go to the list of literary heroes you wrote in the 'Snapshot' exercise earlier on and choose one of their books. Open it at random and copy out a paragraph. That's it. Repeat this process two or three times with different books. It will give you a physical sense of how that writing was built up. While you're doing this, try to pinpoint what it is that appeals to you about that particular piece of writing.

- Is it lavishly descriptive or snappy and concise?
- Is it humorous, sad or frightening?
- Is there a lot of dialogue?
- Is it in the first person, the third person or even the second person?

Now, in fewer than 50 words, try to sum up how this piece of writing makes you feel.

The writing we enjoy most can be a clue to the kind of writing we should create ourselves.

Teachers of other art forms, such as music or painting, are very keen on getting practitioners to copy others' work before they move on to original modes of expression. For obvious reasons, writers should not intentionally copy (plagiarize) other people's work and pass it off as their own, but writing out a piece of a favourite writer's work can help to bring you close to the rhythm and pulse of their writing. It's a way of giving you a physical sense of how they went about building effective passages of writing.

Where to next?

We've discussed the many reasons why you should write and the many benefits it can bring to your life. The next chapter explores how to find ideas and inspiration that will unlock your authentic voice and so begin to create the writing that is distinctively yours.

2

Ideas and inspiration

In this chapter you will learn how to generate and capture ideas, and how to develop them and understand their potential. Many different kinds of creative writing are useful ways of stimulating ideas and inspiration, including free writing, journal or diary writing and 'creative journaling'.

Sometimes the promise of an idea won't be apparent until later – much later, perhaps – maybe years after you first fixed it in note form. It may have seemed flimsy at the time and not worth developing but then something happens that makes it significant. This is why it is so important to get ideas down, wherever you find them – you won't know until later whether they are worthwhile. Your essential tool is a notebook in which to capture your ideas.

Capturing ideas

Your notebook is a weapon for holding your free-range thoughts.

Ideas are tricky little creatures. There are always millions of them around – more than enough for all the writers that have ever been or ever will be. The organic, free-range ideas that run through your head at all sorts of odd times can be speedy, fleeting, even ghostly creatures that are hard to catch. But, if you make sure you have a notebook to hand at all times, you will stand a good chance of corralling them and developing them, so that these stray, wild creatures become fully formed and wholly yours.

Sometimes you will pin these ideas into the pages of your book and, on returning to them, find that they have withered away. Sometimes they were so spindly that they had no chance of growing to a useable size however much you fed or watered them. It's perhaps best to think of ideas, elusive and slippery things that they are, not as thoughts but as *opportunities*. All of them may grow into the thing that helps you produce a great piece of work: something that may even make your name and your reputation. If you don't catch them as they pass, they will disappear. Don't trust that you will remember them or recapture the essence later; you almost certainly won't. If you don't write them down they will vanish, leaving just a sulphuric whiff of frustration and lost opportunity.

Even worse than this, someone else may catch hold of a similar idea (it won't be exactly the same, it may not even be as good) and you will find yourself confronted with the opportunity that became someone else's reputation-cementing piece of work.

Pablo Picasso

'Inspiration does exist, but it has to find you working.'

All ideas have potential

The potential of an idea may develop in your subconscious so that, when you go back to your notes looking for likely candidates, you'll find that what was once a flimsy, weakling of a thought has put on significant muscle while you were away working on something else.

You may well find that, as your writing life develops, you become something of a stationery addict, haunting suppliers in search of notebooks of the perfect size or a make of pen that won't let you down. And it's right that you become obsessive about pens and notebooks; it's right that you fret and worry about paper thickness and the quality of the spines and binding. These are the weapons of the idea hunter. Just as an angler checks that his rods and his wheels and his lines are up to the task of wrestling his prize to the net, so you should ensure that your tools are the kind that will help you make sure no idea ever escapes you.

Focus point

Always, always have a notebook to hand.

Generating your own ideas

Some useful ideas may hurtle out of the sky, or scurry through your mind as if from nowhere. Others you may have to nurture from scratch. Either way, the blank page is always a tyrant to any writer, which is why so many start the day with automatic or free writing – anything to stop the oppression of all that white space.

Free writing

Try your hand at free writing. Set an alarm clock, cellphone or kitchen timer to go off after five minutes and just keep writing for the whole of that time. Don't allow your conscious mind to interfere, just keep writing. Keep your pen moving for the whole period. At least one useful nugget will emerge that might be worked on later. More than this, however, the act of writing, under pressure but without an editor or critic in your head, will help loosen you up for the challenges of your current writing project.

Focus point

Many, many writers are fervent believers in the idea of morning pages: of getting up and writing first thing, before you have had a coffee, showered or washed your face. This, they believe, is when you are most in touch with your subconscious self and able to tap into the rich seams of material that get buried during the working day.

Many writers conscientiously keep dream diaries as repositories of the strange wisdom that comes to us all in the night, and which we can draw on later when creating our polished work.

Keeping a journal

Oscar Wilde

'I never travel without my diary. One should always have something sensational to read in the train.'

Keeping a regular journal or diary is one of the most common pieces of advice given to aspiring writers. Maintaining a record of the day-to-day events of our lives, the places we've been, the people we've met, and the interesting, funny or odd things that happen to us as we move through our lives is excellent writing practice and a great source of ideas. It's also, as we discussed in the previous chapter, a pretty effective antidepressant.

A diary or journal is a private place in which you can write about anything you want. It doesn't have to be a record of what you've done that day. You can write about your memories or ambitions. You can speculate on the love life of the woman over the road. You can make lists of things you love and things you hate. And if you don't have anything to write about, you can just make something up.

CREATIVE JOURNALING

Your journal can be separate from your notebook or you can put everything in one place and make a combination notebook, journal, scrapbook and sketchbook bristling with ideas and observations. It doesn't have to be a series of linear, old-fashioned essays like the ones you used to have to write on Monday mornings at junior school. It can be a place to experiment, to be creative in other ways. You can make collages, get out the old felt-tipped pens or even rediscover finger-painting. Have fun. Make a mess.

Creative journaling is a fast-growing trend, originating in America but catching on all over the world. The idea is that the pages in your journal become a creative playground, visual explorations of your thoughts, ideas and day-to-day life. You definitely don't have to be a talented artist – all you need is a blank book, some basic art materials and a dollop of enthusiasm.

GATHER YOUR MATERIALS

Here are some things you might want to use for your experiments in creative journaling:

- **A notebook or sketchbook**
  If you're going to use paints, you might want to choose one with thick pages, but any blank book will do. If you're feeling especially handy, there are lots of simple tutorials online that

will teach you how to make a journal of your own out of materials you probably already have lying around.

- **Pens**

  Felt-tips, fineliners, highlighters, gel pens and glitter pens can all be picked up relatively cheaply, anywhere from a specialist art supplies shop to your local supermarket, as can watercolour paints, wax crayons and pastels.

- **Magazines for collaging**

  From *Vogue* to the Sunday supplements, start hoarding as many magazines as you can. Don't just cut out pretty pictures – save blocks of colour and texture to use as backgrounds.

- **Vintage paper ephemera**

  Haunt charity shops, second-hand markets and eBay for old newspapers, magazines, comics and sheet music.

- **Personal paper ephemera**

  Ticket stubs, private notes, cards, maps, Polaroid photos and anything else with personal significance are worth saving to display in your journal.

- **Needle and thread**

  You can sew your pages to create beautiful embroidered details, if you are that way inclined.

- **Ink stamps and stickers**

  These can add interesting details to your pages. Japanese washi tape is a delicate, self-adhesive tape that comes in thousands of different colours and patterns and is great for borders and margins.

- **Glue**

  A reliable glue stick is your best friend. You really shouldn't skimp on your glue stick – there's nothing more disheartening than your work falling apart before your eyes.

You'll eventually become something of a magpie, pouncing on shiny paper, whisking the weekend newspapers out of your loved ones' hands before they've even had time to read the comics, and making midnight raids on your kids' pencil cases. Indulge this habit: the more things you have to play with the better.

When you've amassed your stash, get stuck in. Write, illustrate, collage, colour, doodle. Try painting a whole page with watercolours and writing on it before it dries. Use an interesting picture as a prompt for free writing. Copy out a favourite poem or quote and illustrate it with collaged pictures or your own drawings. Do whatever takes your fancy, and if you really make a hash of things, instead of tearing out the page, just paint over it and start again.

Workshop exercise

Pick one of the following prompts and use it to fill a page in your journal or notebook:

- What do colours taste like?
- What do you want right now?
- If I ruled the world …
- My life in scents
- The inside of my head

If you want some inspiration, try a Google image search for 'creative journaling', or search for it on Pinterest.com. You'll also find thousands more prompts to inspire you.

This might well not be your cup of tea. Most adults haven't wielded a wax crayon in decades and might feel a little silly doodling and colouring as if they were back in nursery school. You might find the whole idea a bit frivolous, far from the 'proper' writing you feel you should be doing. You've precious little time for writing as it is, so why should you spend that time messing about with glue sticks and glitter?

The answer, of course, is that you don't have to do it at all if you don't want to. First and foremost, creative journaling should be fun. Many, many adults gave up on drawing and painting when we were told that our pictures of horses didn't look enough like horses to be 'right', to be 'good', that, if anything, they resembled wonky, attenuated dogs. We started to feel ashamed of our efforts and so we stopped trying altogether. We forgot the pure, meditative bliss of making art, that moment of nirvana when your tongue pokes out of the corner of your mouth and the whole world narrows to the tip of your pen.

If you do decide to have a go, you may well find that, after a while, your journal becomes one of the biggest sources of joy in your life.

All forms of creativity are good for us and, if it doesn't sound too terribly 'New Age', experimenting with different methods of creative expression can release an energy in us that can inspire and refresh all aspects of our lives. Creative journaling can be a sneaky back door into the unconscious, unleashing strange and beautiful things we never knew were there. It's a kind of magic.

One final, important point – your creative journal is as private as any other kind. Nobody will ever see it. Just as you shouldn't feel ashamed of anything you write in your personal diary, so you shouldn't be ashamed of your drawing of a wonky horse. He may be wonky, but he's yours.

Using what only you know

There are exercises that can help force ideas to the surface the way that beaters are employed to force game birds into the sky for the hunters to bag.

Writing what you know

Writing what you know is probably the single most common piece of advice handed out to a new writer. And it clearly makes sense, as this exercise shows.

1. Draw up a list of all the jobs you have had.
2. Now write down all the places you have been to in the last five years.
3. Write down all the places you have ever lived.
4. Add to this list all the people whom you have worked with.
5. Write down your hobbies and interests.
6. Write down the names, jobs or interests of all the people you know best.

You should by now have pages and pages of possible material. Suddenly there in front of you are tremendous possibilities for exciting writing that no one else can produce. No one else has quite this collection of characters, settings, stories or experiences. This exercise is a great one for making concrete the sheer wealth of material you have at your fingertips.

There has been an enormous explosion in the number of people researching and writing about their family history. When the 1901 census for England and Wales was first put online in 2002, it received 50 million hits on the first day and crashed. But lists of names and dates and occupations are one thing; what about the real life, the living breathing human beings, behind these connections?

Workshop exercise

In Chapter 1 you made some notes on a family story. Choose a person from that story and try to imagine how you might convey their unique personality to someone who has never met them. Start with the obvious and work inwards.

- Where was she born?
- Where did she live?
- What work did she do?

Now move quickly on to the things that make this person real.

- How did she dress?
- How did she speak?
- What made her laugh? What made her sad?
- Did she have favourite sayings, particular mannerisms or any interesting quirks or habits?

Remember that at this stage we are not counting every word, but we are making every word count.

Including what you don't know

Here is an exercise that stresses the importance of making every word count. It's one I learned from the novelist, short-story writer and screenwriter Mark Illis. It's great as an icebreaker but it also builds on what has gone before and introduces one key new element. This time you are not only writing about what you know best – yourself – but you are also writing what you *don't* know. This is every bit as much of a writer's job as drawing on your own experience. Making stuff up is part of the job description.

USING MAGAZINES AND NEWSPAPERS

These can be great inspirations for your own writing. Usually the headline stories won't be the things that capture your imagination. It can be the smaller snippets that lead you to think 'What if …' which leads on to, 'Let's pretend …' The poet Amanda Dalton kept an article for years about a woman who abandoned her house to live in the garden, building a kind of nest out there from leaves and twigs and bits of rubbish. Her fascination with this woman and the possible reasons for her leading this life grew at last into the sequence of poems called 'Room of Leaves' in her first collection (*How to Disappear*, published by Bloodaxe) and then into an acclaimed radio play. The initial story was just a few lines long but it planted itself in her imagination, growing to fruition over months and years.

Rewrite a newspaper story

Now use the Internet to have a look at a local paper from a foreign country. If you can read another language fluently so much the better, but this exercise works just as well if you look at newspapers from Australia, Canada, the United States, or another English-speaking country. Find a story that seems strange to you and read it carefully.

Now try to rewrite this story as though it happened in the streets of your own town. What would stay the same, what would change? For example, a story about a driver hitting a moose in the Canadian wilderness is obviously going to change dramatically if that moose was hit in Chipping Norton or East Grinstead.

Making the unlikely a reality

Another simple way to get the imagination working is to put yourself in an unlikely situation and to imagine how you might cope. Here is an exercise that was given to me by the short-story writer and novelist Lynne Bryan. The original idea for this exercise came from a tiny story in Lynne's local paper.

Imagine a scenario

Imagine that two people are trapped overnight in a safe. It's a large safe, but nevertheless a small, cramped, stifling place for two people. Your task is to decide:

- Who these two people are
- How they came to be in the safe
- What their relationship is to each other
- What it is like to spend the night in the safe
- What their emotions are upon being rescued in the morning.

Very few people have been trapped in a safe, but all of us can imagine the emotions and sensations this kind of situation could create: boredom, anger, despair, acute anxiety, to name just four.

An extension of the exercise above can be to imagine two figures from history together in this situation or one like it. One writer friend I know is working on a very funny play where the poet Philip Larkin and the filmmaker Quentin Tarantino are stuck together, tied up in a video shop after a heist.

Another variant on this exercise might be to draw up two columns, one containing a list of modern celebrities and another a list of historical figures. Pick one from each list, imagine them meeting in extreme conditions and then describe what might happen.

 ## Everything is material

The essential thing is to be receptive to all the ideas that are out there. For a writer, everything is material, to be processed, transformed, celebrated or examined. Be open to taking inspiration from anywhere, however unlikely a source. There are millions of stories, poems, plays, films and articles in circulation already, but none of them says what only you can say in the way that only you can say it.

Once you start to wander through the world – preferably with your notebook in hand – looking at the world through writer's eyes, you will see that almost everything can be mined for material.

Don't worry too much at this stage about being original. It's far, far better to be good.

David Armstrong

'There are only a certain number of ideas in the world. The good news is that no one knows just how many that number is; the bad news is that people have been mining the seam for a very long time. To write a story, perhaps a novel, what you have to do is conjure a new variation on one of the ideas that has been around for hundreds, if not thousands of years already.

'Take comfort: it's said that Shakespeare didn't have an original idea for any of his plays, but whether he turned to the Romans, the Greeks or English historians, he took that source material and with it he spun pure gold.'

(David Armstrong is a successful writer of crime novels, including Night's Black Angel (HarperCollins)).

Where to next?

In this chapter we've learned that inspiration can come from pretty much anywhere and at any time, so the most vital tool a writer can possess is a notebook in which to capture ideas. Over the coming chapters we'll be looking into different forms of creative writing, to help you decide on the best way to bring these ideas to life.

3

The feature article

There is a huge market for well-written feature articles on an unlimited range of topics. In this chapter you will learn how to choose a subject area for an article from the six most common categories into which successful articles usually fall: specialized knowledge, an unusual angle, humour, topicality, real life and unreal life. You will also learn how to study the market and identify the right publication for your article.

A step-by-step guide to writing your article offers practical advice for producing an interesting piece of writing. Once you are happy with your article, you can approach an editor, and this chapter guides you through this process too, with information on how to avoid the common pitfalls.

What is an article?

An article is not an essay, although it might sometimes resemble one. An article is not a fictional piece, although it may contain anecdotes or stories that are only half true, or which build on the truth in the interest of entertaining a reader. An article is not usually a straightforward opinion piece, although again, it might be. It really depends on whom your article is aimed at.

There are over 650 specialist magazines in the UK, so what constitutes an article might vary considerably. But in case this sounds too daunting, consider the upside: 650 specialist magazines means 650 editors looking to fill a lot of pages every month or every week. It also means that there is a lot of competition between editors for the best material. Sure, they have staff writers to produce regular pieces, but a lot of papers and magazines take work from freelancers and it can be a rewarding way for new writers to learn their craft and earn some income.

 Jeffrey Bernard

'Give someone half a page in a newspaper and they think they own the world.'

 The market

Hundreds of specialist magazines mean hundreds of potential subjects for your articles. This subject is covered in more detail in Lesley Bown and Ann Gawthorpe's *Get Your Articles Published* in the Teach Yourself series.

Choosing a subject

Successful articles usually fall under one of the following headings.

SPECIALIZED KNOWLEDGE

This is any subject about which the writer has a thorough knowledge. The list is literally endless and everyone is an expert in something – for example beekeeping, Budapest, Poland, home education, vegan cookery, computer gaming, women's rugby.

In Chapter 2 you wrote a list that included all the places you've worked, your hobbies and interests and those of the people you know best. This is a goldmine of your unique specialist knowledge that, with a little bit of research, could make fascinating articles.

Expand your knowledge

Make a list of subjects you know nothing about. Pick three and begin to research them. You never know what will pique your interest and provide the inspiration for an article or another piece of writing. Expanding your knowledge is always important.

AN UNUSUAL ANGLE

This involves taking an everyday subject and applying a fresh angle to it. For example, an article about family meals might be too ordinary, but the difficulties of planning them around World Cup viewing might be interesting.

HUMOUR

If you can write a genuinely funny piece, you will find that anything can be your subject.

A rare talent

Write funny pieces regularly and you will find editors beginning to helicopter money over to you. Being funny is incredibly difficult but if you can crack it in the world of newspapers and magazines you might well never need to do a proper job ever again. It really is that rare a talent.

TOPICALITY

Magazine editing is a little like farming: there are definite seasons where stories, like a farmer's crops, have to be planted. There will always be Christmas articles, Hallowe'en articles, summer holiday articles and so on. Anniversaries also need commemorating, whether it is the centenary of a famous (or infamous) person, or a decade since a major event, for example.

Remember to allow yourself enough time to plan for topicality. This book will appear in 2014. The year 2014 means 50 years since the Beatles toured America. It means 25 years since the Hillsborough disaster, 50 years since Muhammad Ali became World Champion, and 25 years since the fall of the Berlin Wall. It means 100 years since the start of the First World War. These are all events that will be extensively revisited in magazines during 2014.

As a writer of features reading this in 2014, you should really be wondering what anniversaries are coming up in 2015 (25 years since Nelson Mandela was freed; ten years since the 7/7 terrorist attacks in London; the tenth anniversary of Hurricane Katrina; 70 years since the liberation of Bergen-Belsen). Furthermore, if you are reading this in spring then you should be planning articles that fit summer and winter.

Record important dates

If you are serious about writing feature articles, you might find it useful to invest in a calendar on which you can record upcoming anniversaries and notable dates. Comb the Internet and you're bound to find at least one event a month that has the potential to make a great article. With all these possibilities recorded on your calendar, you'll never be stuck for an idea again.

Write retrospectively

This exercise involves a bit of time travel. Have a look at today's paper. Pick a story about current events. Now imagine it's ten years from now and try to rewrite the article as a retrospective feature article. How might the future world view these events? What might we have learned from them? What might their consequences be?

REAL LIFE

In the last few years there has been a huge expansion in the market for 'real life' stories. Whole magazines are dedicated to finding and telling the extraordinary true stories of ordinary people. And everyone has these stories – even you. And even if you think you don't, your friends and family do. Ask around. Encourage people to talk to you. Editors are desperate to find the most engaging human stories out there and will pay accordingly.

Your story

Everybody has a story to tell.

Workshop

Now we'll have a closer look at the family story you took notes on in Chapter 1 and developed in Chapter 2, to see whether it has the potential to become an interesting 'real life' article. Of course, you don't have to try to publish it if it's something private that your family wouldn't want to see in a magazine - I don't want to get you in trouble with your mum – but it's a useful exercise to help you see the potential in your story.

- Is the story set in a particularly notable time in history? Was it during the Second World War or at the time of Beatlemania, over the long, hot summer of 1976 or during the Cuban Missile Crisis? If you can find a link between the human story and wider historical events, you've struck gold, especially if, as we've already seen, these events are due an anniversary.
- Where does the story take place? Research the location. Have a look online and see whether you can find any local newspapers from that time to add some genuine local colour. Your article may even be of interest to them.
- Can you relate your story to any 'special interest' magazines? Is it a love story that takes place against the backdrop of motorcycle racing? Was it a funny

UNREAL LIFE

These are the stories about celebrity culture. Often, the magazines that are interested in the extraordinary goings-on in the lives of ordinary people are also the same publications interested in the banal minutiae of celebrity life. And if you can get hold of an extraordinary story about, or an interview with, anyone who is regularly in the public eye, then you will find a ready market for that, too. And they don't have to be top film stars or sportspeople or music stars either. Television presenters, soap actors, weather girls and Internet entrepreneurs can all be worthy of a story. On rare occasions, writers can be fair game, too. Obviously, don't stalk anyone. Go through the proper channels. A courteous letter or email to an agent might have surprising results.

Market study

It is vital to make a close study of the magazines you wish to write for. The author of the first edition of this book, Dianne Doubtfire, tells a story of a writer she knew who once sent an article on karate to a magazine for genteel ladies. 'They should all learn how to defend themselves,' he said. The piece was not commissioned.

The magazines you choose for your market study will be the ones you enjoy reading, the ones that specialize in your own particular interests.

Do your research

Before writing your article, do the following:

- Choose a subject area.
- Choose several magazines that cover this subject.
- Study the length of sample articles in the magazines.

Nothing can really beat counting the actual words in a piece, however tedious this sounds. If you get the length wrong, no matter how brilliant the feature, it won't be used.

Look at the style and content of the articles in several *recent* issues (editors change with almost alarming frequency and with them the editorial policies). Take particular note of the page layout – the way the feature looks on the page.

How many photos are used?

Are text or fact boxes, or sidebars, used to provide the reader with additional information outside the main text? These could be the listing for useful addresses or sources of further information etc. Take this into account when writing your own piece. This will demonstrate to an editor that you are familiar with the style of the magazine.

You should now have plenty of notes on each title. Make sure that you keep them separate for future reference.

Your first article: a step-by-step guide

If you follow the steps outlined below, then you should have an interesting piece of writing that will at least intrigue an editor. Then you can read on to the end of the chapter and go back and correct and redraft in the light of the other notes and suggestions given. At this point, once you are convinced that it is the best you can do, you can send it off.

However, you must realize that you will almost certainly get a rejection the first few times you do this. You may not even receive an acknowledgement for weeks or months. This is normal and you mustn't take it personally. Rejection is part of a writer's life. Developing a thick skin is a necessary part of learning the craft. It might help to think of the end result of all these exercise as being able to gather rejection slips, rather than achieving publication. Each slip then becomes a kind of certificate that shows you are putting in the work, laying the foundations. This then becomes a reward in itself.

1. **Choose your subject,** making sure that it falls under the heading of 'Specialized knowledge', 'Unusual angle', 'Humour', Topicality' or 'Real/unreal life'.

2. **Select a possible market** before you begin. Professional writers usually decide on a market beforehand and, even as an unpractised writer, having a goal in mind will act as a powerful incentive to produce your best work.

3. **Think** about all the points you want to make in your article and jot them down in any order, just as they occur to you.

4. **Sort** through these points, keeping the best but jettisoning any that seem irrelevant or that repeat those you've already got down.

5. **Plan** the order of your points, bearing in mind that it is the first one that must have the most impact. Articles often have their points in the reverse order to other kinds of writing, in that the climax comes first. Your reader must be hooked enough from the start to keep reading.

6. **Write the first draft** and don't worry about style at this point. Just get it down in the order that you have planned. Once you've got it on the page you will see how best to cut it, and where to get rid of any wasted or unnecessary words.

7. **Choose a short, snappy title.**

8. **Double-check all your facts** and make sure that they are up to date. Editors rely on their contributors to know what they are writing about. If you get something wrong, you will struggle to place your work with that editor again.

9. **Put your article in a drawer and wait.** While your article is out of view, a miraculous thing will happen. Your subconscious will work on it and when you retrieve it you will see more mistakes and more clunking prose and more

excess verbiage than you thought possible. If you don't want to twiddle your thumbs during this vital stage, then begin another article or another piece of writing.

10. **Write a second draft.** Rewriting and editing are the hardest, least enjoyable tasks in writing – and probably the most necessary. But if you have waited while your piece ferments out of your sight for a week, then you may find that this important stage is much easier and more enjoyable than you thought it would be. Cutting can be as creative as writing if it is done with brio and courage.

11. **Get some feedback.** If you belong to a writers' group – and you probably should – now is the time to submit your piece to them. Alternatively, get your more candid friends to read it. You won't agree with everything said, but you are likely to get at least one piece of helpful advice and you'll be needing a fresh perspective after spending so much time on revision.

12. **Send a query letter** to the features editor. This letter should be brief and informative, outlining the subject matter and length of the article and the pictures you would provide and so on. If you have specialist knowledge of the subject, say so here. If you do receive a positive response, you will be able to send out your article immediately in the form required – either by post or by email – knowing that it is going to an interested editor rather than on to a slush pile where it will await its turn, along with many others, to be given a cursory glance by the work-experience kid.

13. **Send your work out.** When you feel that your article is ready for submission, type it double-spaced in A4 format (whether you are sending it as a paper copy or as an attachment to an email). Pay attention to detail; editors are busy, professional people and they like their contributors to take similar pains. Don't assume that an editor will look past an untidy manuscript to the gold that lies beneath. He probably won't. He doesn't have time. Some writers are given a lot of leeway: the columnist A. A. Gill, for example, is dyslexic and his manuscripts are littered with spelling mistakes of an original, almost in decipherable nature.

A.A. Gill gets away with it because, well, he is A. A. Gill and has a track record as a wit and critic. You don't – yet.

14. **Be timely with submissions.** Be sure to submit a topical article in good time: two to three months ahead for a weekly magazine, four to six months for a monthly. Many editors buy their Christmas articles in June or earlier.

Practise!

Now you've seen *how* to write a feature article, get writing! The only way to improve is to practise. Try your hand at as many subjects and styles as you can. You don't have to pitch every article you write, but each one will see you improve as a writer.

Mark Twain

'The time to begin writing an article is when you have finished it to your satisfaction. By that time you begin to clearly and logically perceive what it is you really want to say.'

Approaching an editor

Many people are unsure whether to make submissions or send queries by email. The simple answer to this question is, don't. Every magazine listed in the *Writers' and Artists' Yearbook* provides an email address, but this isn't an invitation to bombard the editorial department with story ideas. You may not feel that your politely worded query is part of a bombardment but it will feel like that to the secretary or PA who has literally dozens of similar requests to wade through (in addition to all the other unwanted mail that we all contend with). Traditional snail mail is best in this instance. When you have a track record or a relationship with the editor, then a very brief phone call at an early stage (maybe stage six of the 14 points on the previous pages) might be in order.

PHOTOGRAPHS

The media is increasingly a visual business and photographs will definitely add to the attractiveness of your feature proposal. Don't send negatives; glossy, high-contrast prints will do. Often you can just provide your editor with a list of possible illustrations and, if they like the piece, they will ask you to send the photos as jpeg attachments. Since photos take up a lot of room on a PC, wait until you're asked before you send them, and ensure that you have checked what size and resolution is required. A digital camera is a cheap addition to a writer's armoury and, for the features writer, should never be further away than the notebook.

If illustrations are more appropriate for your article, don't attempt to draw your own. Even if you are a talented artist, an editor may well prefer to use an in-house department.

PAYMENT

Fees vary hugely, depending on the circulation of the magazine. A well-known writer will claim a much higher fee than an unknown one. Fees may well increase once you become a regular contributor.

Focus points

- *Don't* preach.
- *Don't* pad. If your article isn't long enough, write it up for another magazine.
- *Don't* repeat yourself. Readers will lose interest unless every sentence is new.
- *Don't* be discouraged. Each rejection slip is a badge of bravery, so receive it with pride.
- *Don't* be pessimistic. Just as upbeat people have more friends than negative people, so it is with articles. No one wants to feel dejected at the end of a feature and so optimistic, positive pieces – like optimistic, positive people – have better chances.

Changes in printing technology have led to an increasing number of niche and specialist magazines and there are also many online magazines that invite contributions. All this means that there are more outlets for good feature writers than ever before. However, this doesn't make it any easier to get your work out there: there are also more would-be writers than ever before and many of them are putting their work on the Net for free. Web content, from films to music to literature, is easy to get hold of for nothing. There is a whole generation of web-literate consumers who expect to pay little or nothing for material they find on the Internet. For more on this, see Chapter 7, 'Blogging'.

Focus point

Don't neglect the web as a potential marketplace for your work. As years go by and the advertising business diverts more of its expenditure from traditional media, such as television, towards the web, you'll find ad-supported websites looking to cherry-pick the best writers. The half-hearted bloggers will eventually disappear and the cream of the talent will rise to the surface and will always be in demand.

Anthony Clavane

'My tip would be to spend a long time on your intro. After that the rest of the feature should follow naturally. Many journalists talk about a good pay-off line – the last line of the piece – but I believe if you come to the end and you have a great pay-off line maybe substitute it for your intro. Very few people actually read the whole of an article, which is sad but true.'

(Anthony Clavane is chief sports writer for the UK newspaper the Sunday Mirror. *His work has also been published in many other newspapers and magazines.)*

Where to next?

In this chapter we've seen that there is a huge market for well-written feature articles on an unlimited array of subjects and you've been given step-by-step advice to help you plan, research and structure your first attempts. Now we'll move on to the short story, where the facts are what you make them.

4

The short story

In the preface to his book *The Modern Short Story,* H. E. Bates says that 'it is the most difficult and exacting of prose forms'. This is the accepted point of view and yet it is the form that beginners to writing are encouraged to attempt before going on to the long haul of the novel. And there's sense in this. All writers need to learn to write with economy, to draw a character with a few deft strokes of the pen and to pull a reader into a world.

In this chapter you will learn about the scope of the modern short story, some essential ingredients of a successful short story, some common mistakes to avoid and how to generate ideas for a good short story. Here you will also find advice on where to send your stories.

The ingredients

All writers need to learn to write with economy, to draw a reader quickly into a world. With a short story, you also need to know about what to include and what to leave out, and how to create a structure that takes the reader on a journey all the way to a satisfying ending.

To produce an interesting short story you will need:
- an original idea
- believable characters
- a convincing background
- a good opening
- conflict
- suspense
- a sense of shape
- a satisfying ending.

It's obvious, isn't it? And yet these ingredients are by no means always easy to find. And it's not like cooking, where you can do without one of these ingredients or find a simple, more accessible substitute.

 ## Martin Booth

'A short story is like a slap in the face. It must immediately sting, make itself known at once, and it must leave a red mark for hours to come.'

Some common mistakes

The most common mistake is to try to be too dramatic. Thinking that a short story must be high impact, writers are drawn to violence and suffering. Novice writers often try to make an impression by shock. It's a tactic best avoided, however. Everyone tends to recoil from an explosion and readers are no different when they see blood and guts spilled too visibly on to the page. They do what most people do: they avert their eyes. Unless a new writer is very skilled, it will be hard to persuade a reader to be led down the darkest alleyways.

Another mistake is to offer up as a story the unadulterated anecdote. If your job means you mix with a lot of people, you are bound to have a fund of funny stories, but what works as a funny story at a party doesn't always work on the page. Similarly, we all know people who are great raconteurs in the pub or around a dinner-party table, but it does not follow that any of their tales would work in a written form without a great deal of revision.

The same is true of those writers who simply give us their unvarnished personal experiences, however shocking or powerful these have been. This is not to decry the value of writing these down. Often they can be the springboard for producing honed and developed pieces. And, in any case, making sense of our own lives is at least part of the point of writing – all writing.

However, a written story needs to be crafted, with care and thought. Readers are far more acute and unforgiving than an audience at a social gathering.

A short story must be crafted

Even a very good anecdote will not have the power of a well-worked story when transferred directly to the page. It will need something more. It will need the application of craft.

Finding short-story ideas

In Chapter 2 we talked about how ideas need to be hunted down and corralled. We owe it to ourselves to treat our ideas seriously and as important. You should therefore, by now, have plenty of rough ideas in your notebook and a file of odd incidents culled from local papers and magazines.

The germ of a short story could also come from an overheard conversation or a fragment of something that was on television or the radio. Or you could try one of the following exercises in order to generate still more ideas for short stories. They are both good ways of involving other people in your writing. The more involved they feel, the more supportive they are likely to be, and your life as a writer is likely to be much easier if your partner, friends and family all feel included in your efforts.

Use secrets

This is a well-known exercise used by many writers and teachers to get their imagination going. It seems particularly suitable for the short-story form. You will need some close friends to help you. Better still, the members of your writing group could help.

Everyone writes down a secret on a piece of paper, which they fold up and place in a hat, a bag or a box. Each person draws out a secret and uses it as a springboard for writing a story. If you are doing this in a writing group, you should all meet again and swap the stories you developed from each other's secrets.

Use photographs

Whatever kind of writer you are, it's a good idea to get into the habit of collecting photographs and postcards. Snap up anything that grabs your eye and put it safely in a box somewhere. On a day when the ideas just don't seem to want to come, you can go to the box and pick out a photo at random. It's probably best to choose one that you collected so long ago that you had forgotten you'd got it.

Spend ten minutes free-writing about the photograph. Then use the photo – or a detail from it – as a starting point for your story.

Finding believable characters

The most important task for the short-story writer is to choose the right central character. Unlike a novel, a short story usually revolves around one person whose problem becomes increasingly interesting. The reader needs to know and care about this person and so it is probably helpful to restrict yourself to a single viewpoint throughout the story. In other words, see everything through one character's eyes. Make sure, in choosing your character, that *you* at least sympathize with their plight. If you don't, then it is unlikely that any of your readers will care either.

At this stage in your writing career, it might be a good idea to write using the first person. Your readers are possibly more likely to identify more easily with an 'I' character.

Focus point

Dialogue is essential in a short story. People reveal themselves by the things they say and readers will feel that they know your characters far better if they can hear their unique voices.

Short stories are where eccentrics can often find a suitable fictional home. Here is an exercise that has often been used very effectively at the Arvon Centre at Lumb Bank in Yorkshire. It is an excellent one for finding characters and their voices.

Gather material

Take yourself off into your nearest town or village. Spend some time really looking at your fellow citizens. Find someone as different from you as possible – someone much older, say, or much younger. Follow them, keeping a discreet distance but staying close enough to be able to watch how they move. If they are with companions, try to overhear what they say. You could even begin this exercise in a café, overhearing what your fellow customers are talking about and then following a selected target as he or she leaves the premises. Try to gather as much information about your target's life as you can and then, safely back at home, make some detailed notes. This should give you enough material on which to base a central character.

A convincing background

Your characters should move in a realistic setting, though you don't want to spend a lot of time evoking it. Your job as a short-story writer is to take your readers into the imaginary world and make them believe in it immediately.

It is probably a good idea to choose the kind of setting you know well. Think about evoking all the senses, not just the visual; smells and sounds are as important as the way things look. Taste and touch can be as evocative, too.

William Kennedy

'Without a sense of place the work is often reduced to a cry of voices in empty rooms, a literature of the self, at its best poetic music; at its worst a thin gruel of the ego.'

A good opening

A good short story needs to get going quickly. Your main character needs to make an appearance straight away. You must arouse your reader's curiosity within the first page. Ideally, the first paragraph should be arresting. If the story doesn't really get going until page three, then throw away pages one and two. You as a writer might need the first two pages, but the reader doesn't.

Here are three openings to contemporary short stories that show how it is done. The first is from 'Capacity' by the American writer Marjorie Sandor, who won the National Jewish Book Award in 2005. The second is from 'Are These Actual Miles?' by Raymond Carver. And the third is the opening of the story 'Think Like a Bee' by Jo Verity, winner of the Richard and Judy short story competition in 2004. All three of these openings entice a reader into a compelling, imaginative world and hint at dramas still to come.

Marjorie Sandor

'By the time she was eleven, the house was deep in age-old quiet. She had tender breasts already and, my God, what looked like hips, said the Shapiro aunts, turning her this way and that in the kitchen. Her mother and the aunts kept her well surrounded: no dark fact could break into this picture, dirty it up or confuse it. But it was 1936 and her father's store was in trouble, and something else was wrong. His eyesight

was failing, and he got up to pee five times a night. Nobody spoke of it. The aunts swarmed in her mother's parlour, clutching Clara to their bosoms, giving her big smacking kisses. "Doll," they called her, and "Cutie-pie", words that didn't suit her then, that never would. She felt, at the time, shunned by life, as if it didn't think her worth the effort, and was deliberately keeping away.'

Raymond Carver

'Fact is the car needs to be sold in a hurry, and Leo sends Toni out to do it. Toni is smart and has personality. She used to sell children's encyclopedias door-to-door. She signed him up, even though he didn't have kids. Afterward, Leo asked her for a date, and the date led to this. This deal has to be cash, and it has to be done tonight. Tomorrow somebody they owe might slap a lien on the car. Monday they'll be in court, home free – but word on them went out yesterday when their lawyer mailed the letters of intention. The hearing on Monday is nothing to worry about, the lawyer has said. They'll be asked some questions, and they'll sign some papers, and that's it. But sell the convertible, he said – today, tonight. They can hold on to the little car, Leo's car, no problem. But they go into court with that big convertible, the court will take it, and that's that.'

Jo Verity

'Esther didn't recognize the elderly man standing at the door. A stranger on the step after dark would normally cause her heart to race but this one looked pretty harmless.

"Good evening, Mrs Feldman. Esther." Well, he certainly knew who she was. "I was in the neighbourhood and I recalled that your house was on Jenckes Street. So I figured that if I knocked on every sixth door, the probability was that

I'd track you down sooner or later. I only had to call at nine houses. Not bad." He paused and while she wrestled with the mathematics of the door-to-door enquiry, he added "It's Stanley. Stanley Johnson? Thanksgiving Day? Remember?"

'A recollection lay buried somewhere in her memory but, before she had time to dig it out the draught from the open door caught the curtains and they billowed out, flicking a vase of crimson gladioli off the window ledge in the living room. The two of them knelt, gathering up broken glass, mopping up stale water, and she was grateful that this little guy, whoever he was, had turned up out of the blue.'

Write the next paragraph

Reread the openings above. Select one and try to write the next paragraph. When you are next in the library, see whether you can read the story to see how close you were. Did the story move in unexpected directions? Copying a writer's style directly like this can be a good way to learn. You might even prefer your own next paragraph, which would be quite a confidence boost!

Conflict

'Happiness writes white,' they say. In other words, contentment rarely makes for powerful stories. In a piece of short fiction, you will need to ensure that your characters face problems from the start. They should be beset with difficulties and enemies and conflict. The difficulty needn't be melodramatic – it could be as simple as someone occupying your character's favourite seat in the local pub – but it should disturb them and disrupt their rhythm.

Here is an exercise from the American Orange prize-winner Suzanne Berne. It's designed to allow you to develop conflict without succumbing to the temptation to become overblown.

Small events, big conflict

Describe a ritual that you have. Everyone has rituals, things they do to control their environment. Your ritual might be the way you make tea, or a routine you have when going to work – something you do in more or less the same order at more or less the same time. Now imagine a break in that routine. What happens if the kettle doesn't work or the bus breaks down? Imagine the chain of events that might develop from there. Then imagine that you meet the person who has caused this disruption to your day. What might happen then? This is a good exercise for making it clear how small events can produce big emotional conflict.

Shape

Put simply, this means that your story should have a beginning, a middle and an end. The beginning sets the scene, introduces the characters and poses the problem. The middle develops the action and explores the world of the story; and the end resolves the dilemmas of the central characters, for better or worse. Your task is to make sure that everything is relevant to the development of the story – and to jettison everything that might be irrelevant. Be hard on yourself and on your story.

Suspense

Your story should be plausible but never predictable. Having hooked your readers with a powerful beginning or beguiling opening, you need to prevent them wriggling off. Avoid the temptation to depart from your main storyline or get sucked into giving away too much backstory about your characters. You might need to know where they went to school or how they met their first boyfriend but, unless it's absolutely essential to the story, your reader probably doesn't. It's about building tension: making the reader worry about what will happen next.

A good way to sketch out a plot is to keep building on that first dramatic scene. Each scene should suggest another. A lot of writers plan their plots in advance before they write a word. And it's probably sensible. You should also give your characters choices as the story progresses. Offer them different roads to take. Sometimes these should be the wrong roads. Your reader should want to scream at your characters, or to shake them. We should fall in love with some and be irritated by others, but feel at least a little sympathy for all of them. A good way to think about constructing a storyline is to imagine that your job as a writer is to get your characters stuck up a tree, to throw rocks at them and then to get them down again.

We'll return to the importance of a strong storyline later in this book, but its impact can't be overestimated. It is, after all, the story that keeps the readers interested rather than your beautiful prose.

 ## Moving the story along

Every paragraph, every line, should move the story along. If it doesn't do that, it hasn't earned its place, however euphonic it is.

A satisfying ending

The ending doesn't need to be a happy one. Nor does it have to be one that ties up all the characters' relationships. It is perfectly possible to have a well-written, satisfying ending that leaves possibilities open. With all stories, it is important that you leave the reader some of the work to do. Readers are smart and want to be able to guess what is going to happen to the characters. As the story progresses, you will want to wrong-foot them and surprise them. But resist the temptation at the end to tell them everything that happens to the characters. Leave them to reflect and to wonder about the characters' futures.

You don't necessarily have to have a dramatic twist, either. That can look contrived. Unless it is very skilfully done, it will just irritate a reader. While your story should end with some sort of emotional release for the reader, try to avoid doing this with a death. If you kill off your viewpoint character, you will disconcert the reader, who will wonder who is telling the story. And if you kill off the hero, or a character that the reader has come to like or identify with, then you cause a little death in the heart of the reader, too.

And there is nothing like finishing a piece to encourage a writer to move on and develop further.

When deaths occur

As a general rule, when deaths occur in short stories they should happen at the beginning rather than at the end.

The first 500 words

Choose a theme and a central character for a short story. Make notes for a beginning, a middle and an end and write the first 500 words. You should by now have some substantial material from previous exercises that you can use.

Where to send your story

The first place to send your completed short story should be to a drawer. Print it off and leave it to sit and simmer for several weeks. While your story is lying apparently dormant in that drawer, it will actually be cooking somewhere in your subconscious. When you do finally return to it, you will be amazed by how many flaws you find. Don't be depressed or downhearted by this; it's a necessary part of the process. Read your story through carefully, making notes in the margins.

Always, always, always edit from a hard copy. Don't try to edit on screen. You'll miss things. The experience of reading on screen is very different from reading a printed page and it makes sense to come to your work in the same way as your reader will.

Workshop exercise

Here are some questions to ask yourself as you reflect on your story:

1. Does the action start straight away, or is there some preamble that could be cut?

2. Do you have any stray adverbs or adjectives that aren't earning their keep?

3. In *On Writing: A Memoir of the Craft,* Stephen King reveals his formula for editing his work – the second draft is the first draft, minus 10 per cent. Will losing 10 per cent of your word count tighten your story?

4. Read your story out loud. Are there any passages that seem to 'clunk'? Pay particular attention to dialogue. Does it sound natural?

5. Ask someone else to read your story and give you feedback. Can they summarize the story? Did they have a clear idea of what was happening? Could they identify the theme of the story, if there was one? Did they find the ending satisfying?

Once you've edited and revised and – probably – completely redrafted your story, send it back to the drawer to simmer some more and then take it out and go through the editing, revising and redrafting process all over again. You might want to do this a few times.

When you are finally happy with your story, you can start finding outlets for it. Don't feel nervous about this. You've worked hard, and, if you've followed all the advice and exercises in this chapter, then you have worked very hard indeed, and a tale that you have grown, developed and nurtured over all these weeks and months deserves a readership. It is very possible, likely even, that the first few stories you send out will attract rejections, but remember that I am choosing to see these as scars and battle honours, necessary bruises on the way to ultimate success.

MAGAZINES

The best place to look for outlets is in the *Writers' and Artists' Yearbook* (A & C Black), which contains the addresses of more or less anyone a writer might ever find useful, including those magazines that publish short stories.

A few of the major magazines are listed here. Once again, it makes sense to study the magazine before you submit your work.

Name	Address	Editor
Aesthetica	PO Box 371 York YO23 1WL Tel: 01904 479168 Email: info@aestheticamagazine.com	Cherie Federico
Ambit	17 Priory Gardens London N6 5QY Website: www.ambitmagazine.co.uk	Briony Bax
Mslexia	PO Box 656 Newcastle upon Tyne NE99 1PZ Tel: 0191 261 6636 Email: postbag@mslexia.demon.co.uk Website: www.mslexia.co.uk	Guest editors
Stand	School of English, University of Leeds Leeds LS2 9JT Tel: 0113 233 4794 Department of English Virginia Commonwealth University Richmond, VA 23284-2005 USA Email: dlatane@vcu.edu Website: www.standmagazine.org	Jon Glover
Staple	114–16 St Stephen's Road Nottingham NG2 4JS Website: www.staplemagazine.wordpress.com	Wayne Burrows

Two publishers in this country specialize in the short story – look out for their anthologies and subscribe to their newsletters so that you know when they are asking for submissions:

Name	Address
Comma Press	3rd Floor, 24 Lever Street, Northern Quarter Manchester M1 1DW Website: www.commapress.co.uk
Salt Publishing	PO Box 937 Great Wilbraham Cambridge CB1 5JX Website: www.saltpublishing.com

The short-story competition

Despite the dedicated work by editors like Ra Page at Comma and Chris Hamilton-Emory at Salt, the fact remains that there are only a handful of short-story outlets, their editors often drowning in manuscripts and physically unable to read each one, never mind publish them all. One online monthly magazine restricts its writers to one published story every three years in order to spread around the opportunities it offers!

One way in which your work can be read is through a short-story competition. There are many of these now, with prizes ranging from a few pounds to several thousands of pounds, and it can be a practical way to test how your writing is progressing. Writers should be collecting rejection slips the way that Prussian officers collected duelling scars, and short-story writers should approach competitions in the same way. Winning is only part of the point; their real function is to stimulate you to produce new work.

This is not the same as urging you to send in any old thing. Each competition is a mountain to be conquered and, as a mountaineer setting out on a new expedition, it pays to be thoroughly and properly prepared.

 Focus point

If you have to pay a fee to enter it, a competition may be a simple fundraiser for the organizers, while others carry considerable weight and heft. Winning the Bridport Prize, for example, gave Kate Atkinson a great deal of enhanced standing in the literary world. As a crude rule, the higher the prize money the more respected the prize. This also means that the competition will be stiffer, of course!

As a beginner, you might want to look at the less valuable prizes first. These are likely to attract fewer entries and, with luck, the judges will be able to spend more time considering each story. Don't just look at the monetary value of the prizes, however. How long the competition has been established is also an important indication of how respected it is.

When entering a competition, make sure that you research the judges, too. Try to read some of their work. If you can't muster any enthusiasm for their work, there has to be a fair chance that you and they are not on the same wavelength.

Some competitions use a filter system, where the named judges select only from a shortlist chosen by others. If a writers' group is holding a competition, and many of the smaller ones do, it is very likely that the filter judges will be drawn from that group. It makes sense therefore to check out the group. How long has it been established? How many members does it have? Have they published any group pamphlets or anthologies? If so, it might be a good idea to have a look at the kind of work they produce.

Certainly, you absolutely must get hold of any anthologies of winning and shortlisted entries from previous competitions. This is the best way to see what the standard is and whether or not it is worth the outlay. It is also a form of good manners. You want people to read your stories, so it is only right to read the work of those who have successfully gone before. And, as already mentioned, reading the work of others is the quickest way to improve as a writer. One of the great things about writing is that we can choose our own mentors. It doesn't even matter if they are dead! We can study their works and learn at the knee of the masters and mistresses of the craft at our leisure.

It ought to go without saying, but read the competition rules and entry forms carefully. Do exactly what they ask and double-check before you post off the entry. Check the small print, too. Make sure that copyright eventually returns to the author, even if the competition organizers have copyright for a short while in order to use the piece in an anthology or for publicity purposes, which is fair enough.

Don't try to amend your entry after you have submitted it. There's really no point. If the story doesn't go places, redo it with the corrections and amendments for another competition at another time.

Here is a list of the major regular short-story competitions, but there are others springing up all the time. Keep an eye on magazines like

Mslexia (ostensibly just for women but all writers should consider a subscription to this magazine) that produce a regular list of competitions. In addition, The Book Trust provides a comprehensive A to Z of annual awards and prizes. Visit www.booktrust.org.uk.

Major short story competitions include the following:

Name	Address	Prize
The Bridport Prize Short story and poetry categories. Closing date 30 June each year.	Bridport Arts Centre, South Street, Bridport Dorset DT6 3NR Website: www.bridportprize.org.uk	£5,000
Fish Short Story Prize	Fish Publishing, Durrus, Bantry Co. Cork, Republic of Ireland Email: info@fishpublishing.com Website: www.fishpublishing.com	€10,000
***The Lady* Short Story Competition** Open to all. Details published in *The Lady*.	*The Lady* 39–40 Bedford Street London WC2E 9ER Website: www.lady.co.uk/	£1,000
Bryan Macmahon Short Story Award	*Writers' Week* 24 The Square, Listowel Co. Kerry, Republic of Ireland Tel: (353) 6821074 Email: info@writersweek.ie Website: www.writersweek.ie	£2,000
National Short Story Prize Entrants must be published authors.	Booktrust, Bookhouse 45 East Hill London SW18 2QZ Email: Hannah@booktrust.org.uk Website: www.theshortstory.org.uk/prizes	£15,000 for the winning story, £3,000 for the runner-up and £500 for the three other shortlisted stories.
The Tom-Gallon Trust Award and the Olive Cook Prize For fiction writers of limited means who have had at least one short story accepted for publication. Both awards are biennial and awarded in alternate years. Closing date 31 October each year.	Awards Secretary The Society of Authors 84 Drayton Gardens, London SW10 9SB Tel: 020 7373 6642 Email: info@societyofauthors.org Website: www.societyofauthors.org	£1,000

Enter a competition

Choose one of the competitions above and check the word-count rules. Take your short story out of its drawer and edit it down to fit the parameters of the competition. Now submit it – you never know.

Jo Verity

'Start as near to the end of your story as possible. No waffle about blue skies and buzzing bees – unless they sting someone. Draw your reader in quickly with dialogue or an interesting observation. Assume an "intelligent reader". Don't hand them everything on a plate. Make them do some of the work – they'll feel more committed. When you think you've finished, try knocking off the last sentence. If the story still works, why is it there?'

(In addition to her prize-winning short stories, Jo Verity is the author of the novels Bells *and* Sweets from Morocco *(both Honno).)*

Where to next?

In this chapter we've seen that short stories aren't any easier than novels just because they're shorter, but by following the advice and tips here you should still manage to create something you're proud of. In the next chapter we'll turn to a burgeoning field in contemporary creative writing – creative non-fiction.

5

Creative non-fiction

Creative non-fiction is becoming the most widely used term
to cover memoir, biography, autobiography, travel writing
and writing about historical events. All these kinds of writing
have always been popular, but in recent years there has been
an increase in demand for works in these genres. More than
ever, audiences seem to crave 'authenticity' and 'real life'.

In order to work, all non-fiction requires the same creative
writing skills as those of fiction. It needs a solid structure, a
compelling narrative voice and a clear connection of ideas.
The 'truth' of your work will not necessarily be what engages
your readers; it will be how well you present that truth. In
this chapter you will learn about the requirements of creative
non-fiction, how to find a subject and think about structure,
how to do research and how to write a proposal.

Why become a creative non-fiction writer?

Everyone tells real-life stories. Everyone comes home from even the simplest journey with an anecdote to tell. It might be something that happened to them or something they saw; or it might be a funny story told to them in a shop or at work. We are a storytelling species. Stories are how we make sense of the world around us. For most people, their stories are true; they are real things that happened to real people in real places. Nevertheless, everyone – often without realizing it – crafts their story, shaping it so that it becomes more entertaining for the listener. In this way, everyone already has the basics for producing great non-fiction work instinctively. Some people will be better at it than others, just as some people are naturally faster than others, but we all have the basic tools and can develop this native ability.

Everyone has had important, dramatic, surprising things happen to them. Equally, every family history is filled with characters and dramas: little legends that demand telling. And the broad sweep of history, too, features people who have been forgotten and neglected, people whose stories deserve retelling for new audiences. As the writer of these stories, whether your own or other people's, you will gradually become an expert in some area of life. Your area of expertise might be narrow, but nevertheless part of the appeal of becoming a writer of non-fiction is that you will be the authority on the stories you choose to tell.

 George Meredith

'Memoirs: The backstairs of history.'

Finding a subject

You perhaps already have an idea of the story you want to write. Perhaps you lived through an era or in a place others know little about, or you just want to get your life down so that others in your family – children or grandchildren, for example – understand what those times were like for you. Whatever the reason, you are probably excited by the idea of writing an autobiography.

It might be that there are family legends – tales passed down from your own parents and other older relatives – that you want to verify. There might be family characters whose lives seem worth exploring in more detail: a great-great-uncle in the Royal Flying Corps, a great-great-aunt who was one of the original suffragettes. You might have an ancestor who sailed to America in search of a better life or who was fleeing persecution or economic hardship. One person who attended a writing course at the Ted Hughes Arvon Centre wanted to tell the story of her great-grandmother, the original inspiration for the Alice in Wonderland stories. Another was inspired by finding his grandfather's wartime diaries that recorded his time as a Battle of Britain fighter pilot.

Other writers have ambitions that are slightly larger in scope. One who came to our writing centre wanted to tell the story of a First World War poet, a contemporary of Owen and Sassoon, who she felt had been unjustly ignored and about whom little seemed to be known. Other people are excited by the idea of travel and reflecting on their travels for themselves and for others.

Federico Fellini

'All art is autobiographical. The pearl is the oyster's autobiography.'

Exploring creative avenues

This is a similar exercise to one we did in Chapter 2, 'Ideas and inspirations', but it is a variation that might help show you the huge range of creative avenues open to you.

Make a simple timeline of all the key moments in your life. You might begin with the most obvious: your birth.

You might end up with something like this:

Nicola Lawson

- Born 1968 Watford
- Began at Bash Street Infants, Watford, September 1973
- Moved to Nigeria for Dad's work, August 1976
- Returned to Watford July 1981, attended Enid Blyton High School
- Met Danny Finch who became first boyfriend; beginning of Wild Years
- June 1986 – dropped out of High School, left home
- June 1988 – married Guy Peters
- September 1989 – first child Tamara born
- September 1992 – divorced Guy Peters, attended access course at local college
- October 1994 – enrolled at Greenwich University
- June 1997 – graduated with first-class honours in History
- September 1997 – got job with Greenwich Museum Service
- Attended evening classes in life-drawing where met Barry Rogerson
- August 1999 – married Barry Rogerson
- July 2001 – second child Elliot born
- October 2003 – moved to Spain with Barry to run a bar
- February 2005 – returned to England to look after mother who was seriously ill
- February 2006 – sold bar, returned to England. At Luton airport daughter Tamara spotted by modelling agent and given contract one month later
- February 2007 – picked up copy of *Vogue* with Tamara on the front cover. Decide to write book about year as mother of aspiring model.

There's a lot here, and a lot that might interest a reader. What was life like for someone spending a large part of her childhood in Nigeria? For example, what exactly did Nicola do in her 'Wild Years'? What prompted Nicola to return to education? Why did her first marriage fail? What was Guy Peters like? What attracted her to Barry Rogerson? Was he another student on the course?

The teacher? The model? What was life like in Spain as a bar owner who was also trying to bring up a toddler? Why did she give up work with the Museum Service? Did she take her children with her when she went back to look after her mum? Did her mother recover and what was wrong with her anyway?

And then there are the big questions posed by the facts towards the end of Nicola's timeline: how did the modelling agent approach her daughter? What was Nicola's reaction? Was she suspicious? Delighted? And what were the stresses and strains of being plunged into that world? How did their lives change? How did Tamara cope with it all? What does Nicola feel about the modelling industry? Did she meet any interesting people? What does the future hold for the family now?

No doubt your own timeline will be at least as interesting as this one and throw up as many questions and provide as many possibilities for future work. What is clear, though, is that if Nicola was telling her life story she probably wouldn't want to start right at the beginning. She herself made the decision that the most interesting thing for her to write about was the whole experience of becoming the mother of a young model.

She took an incident that happened late on in her timeline and took that as the subject of her first book. If she does it well, that first book will be a mixture of memoir, a study of the fashion and modelling industries, and a biography of her daughter's short life. If she pulls it off, it'll be a thought-provoking, entertaining read.

There were other avenues she could have gone down, of course. For example, her mother, it so happens, was the niece of the writer Georgina Basket, who produced popular detective novels in the 1940s. This was the same Georgina Basket who, family legend has it, was rumoured to have been a spy during the Second World War and was dropped by parachute several times into occupied France in order to pass important messages to the Resistance.

She could also have written about the area of Spain where she and her second husband ran a bar. Barry and Nicola and their children were the only English people living in a small town high in the Pyrenees and, as such, were objects of much curiosity. Fitting into the local community was often a challenge, particularly as they didn't speak the language and Barry never saw a reason to. Ultimately, however, the experience was rewarding despite all the difficult and comical moments along the way. They were all were sad to leave and one of the first things Tamara did when she became a successful model was to buy a cottage in the town.

Nicola could also have written about her experience of getting divorced from Guy Peters, which was astonishingly amicable and, she feels, could easily be a template for others going through similarly awkward situations. Perhaps her next book will be a manual for a civilized divorce. Or she could have written about the eminent Victorian explorer and philanthropist Lady Freeborn of Whittlesea, whose letters she came across while studying for her dissertation at Greenwich University and whom she has always wanted to research.

Any moderately active life will furnish similar possibilities.

Shape and structure

The most obvious structure for a memoir or a biography is that suggested by William Shakespeare at the beginning of *As You Like It*. You must know it. It's the 'Seven Ages of Man' sonnet that begins with 'All the world's a Stage/And all the men and women merely players'.

Shakespeare's Seven Ages begins with the infant 'mewling and puking in the nurse's arms' and moves on through the schoolboy, the lover, the soldier, the justice, and the 'lean and slippered pantaloon', before the seventh age of second childishness 'sans teeth, sans eyes, sans everything'.

It is easy to imagine the memoirist or the biographer looking back from the point of view of the sixth or even seventh age, and beginning their recollections with all that mewling and puking before moving on steadily through the other ages. And it might easily be quite dull. In any case, is the birth of the subject even the start of his story? In the novel *Tristram Shandy* the narrator finds himself compelled to begin his life story from the moment of his conception, which means he has to describe the childhood of his parents and so on. The story hardly gets started. A modern reader wants to be pulled into the story straight away.

The importance of the opening

Possibly the most important thing about any piece of writing is the opening and this is just as true for a piece of non-fiction writing as it is for a novel.

The following exercise might help give you an insight into how you might shape your non-fiction work.

Write about your day

Think of all the things you did yesterday. Make a list, starting with getting up and ending with going to bed. Now choose the most interesting thing that happened yesterday and write that down in as much detail as you can. I guarantee that at least one interesting thing happened yesterday. Try to capture it all. Describe the characters involved and where they were. Just stick to the who, the what, the where and the why. Keep it short.

Now complete this next exercise, which focuses on one area of the timeline.

Workshop exercise

Go back to your timeline and pick a pivotal moment in your life, one incident that seemed to sum up where your life was going. It might be a row with a parent, a proposal of marriage, a stag or hen night, a job interview, the birth of a child or your arrival in a foreign country. The incident may be large or small, but the important thing is that it is one vivid episode that has stayed with you for many years. Write it up as if you were telling it for the first time to an interested person who doesn't know you or anything about the people involved. Write it in the present tense as though the event is happening right now.

Begin with the words 'I am ...' and carry on from there. Try to set the scene; make the readers really feel like witnesses.

For example:

'I am sitting in my father's chair, the leather armchair with the odd high back. We are waiting for him to come home, my mother and I. I have something important to say.'

Here are some questions to guide you as you are thinking about this piece:

1. **Where** does this incident take place? Make some notes on the setting, a list of little details you can use to imbue your writing with an authentic sense of place.

2. **When** did this happen? You can transport your readers back in time with the smallest of details – for example, were the ladies on the hen night drinking Babycham or WKD?

3. **Who** was involved? Characterization is as important in autobiography as it is in fiction. See Chapter 10, 'Taking your novel further', for more notes and exercises to help you develop your characters.

4. **What** were the consequences? What did you learn from this incident? Do you look back on it and laugh or cry? Do you cringe? These are the emotions you want to elicit from your readers.

5. **Why** is this incident so important to you and your life? How did it shape you? What did you learn from it? Why would it be interesting to other people?

One point of this exercise is to show you that your memoir or biography needn't necessarily begin at the beginning and move forward from there. That is, of course, one way to do it, but it might be an idea to start with something that reveals something about the character, or something that foreshadows the kind of person your subject became.

DIFFERENT VIEWPOINTS

Here is another exercise designed to help you think about the structure of a piece of creative non-fiction.

Be selective

Imagine that it is your funeral. Make notes about who will be there and who might be missing. Now imagine that a good friend is standing up to deliver the eulogy. What might they say about you? What stories might they tell, designed to show your character in all its eccentric humanity? (We already know that you are eccentric because you have decided to become a creative writer!) Crucially, what might they leave out in telling your story to the assembled congregation?

Being selective is a skill of all writing and it is especially true of non-fiction writing. What not to write is every bit as important as deciding what to put in and where. At a funeral, each speaker has just a few minutes to deliver a monologue about the deceased, so your eulogy to yourself will need to be just a few pages long but has still to cover the most important facts of your life and to tell a few good stories, too. It's not easy is it? But it's possibly the most useful exercise in structure there is, and you may well find out something about yourself as well.

If you find the idea of writing your own funeral address too depressing, you could try preparing a best man's speech for your own wedding, or a father's speech if you are a bride. The problems are still the same: what goes in, what stays out and what order do you place the events in?

Of course the exercise above assumes that you will present yourself in a reasonably good light. Best-man speeches can be teasing or risqué, but are usually affectionate. Funeral speeches are nearly always respectful. It could be an interesting exercise to try it again from the point of view of someone who doesn't like you much. You might be one of those fortunate few who have managed to get through life without making enemies, but that is not true for most of us. Most of us have ex-wives, ex-lovers, ex-friends or ex-colleagues who we know would not be all that flattering if they had the chance to write down their true feelings about us. If writing is, as Hemingway said it was, a case of writing 'hard about what hurts', then we should try to put ourselves in the shoes of someone who doesn't share our benign view of ourselves.

 ## Consider various viewpoints

Imagine that someone who you suspect doesn't like you much is writing you a letter about the way you have lived your life. What are they going to say? What will they put in that the funeral orator or best man might leave out? Make notes and then write the letter, trying to capture your former friend's way of speaking. Try to inhabit their mindset as much as possible.

The reason for doing this exercise is to reinforce the obvious point that there are always at least two sides to every story and it's your duty as a biographer or an autobiographer to acknowledge other points of view. However, don't allow the need for balance to cause you to lose focus – you don't want to confuse your readers, and it is absolutely OK to have a strong consistent argument.

Focus point

No one is interested in hearing just about triumphs and successes or in simply learning about what a wonderful chap the person you are writing about is or was. They want the darker, harder truths, too.

Being flexible

Lives are awkward, restless creatures. They simply won't stand still and they resist being encased into a rigid cage no matter how carefully we have designed it. As you research the life, place or period you have decided to write about, you will find that your preconceptions are challenged all the time. Your research may well lead you off into places where you didn't expect to go. Those characters you thought might be heroes will turn out to be not quite as heroic as you had thought, the villains not quite so villainous. Happy childhoods may turn out to have been miserable all along. Your own past actions may not stand up to much close scrutiny.

It is in this gap between assumptions and realities that the real fun of being a creative non-fiction writer lies. It can be unsettling. But, like a good detective, you have to go wherever the evidence takes you. This means that your plan must be flexible, adaptable. You must be able to keep an open mind and to change it when necessary. It' s no good being like the stubborn politician who thinks they are showing courage when they announce that they are not for turning, or that they have no reverse gear. A vehicle that can't turn round or backtrack when circumstances demand it is more or less useless. And so is a biographer.

Use all the evidence

Here is a little exercise in flexibility. Write down something that happened to you when you were a child. It doesn't need to be a big thing. It can be the day you fell off your bike. But when you've written down the facts as you know them, call up someone else in your family who might know a little about the incident. Read them what you've written and ask if they have anything to add. They almost certainly will. Now rewrite the incident including any new facts or details you have been given. In any piece of memoir writing or biography, this kind of experience will occur frequently and it is best to accept new information gracefully and alter your plan, rather than trying to make it fit your established world view.

Beginning your research

With any kind of research-based project, the best places to start are the most obvious. Begin with personal contacts. Then you can make use of the Internet and other sources such as your library and your public records office.

PERSONAL CONTACTS

If it is an autobiography you are working on, your family and friends will be the first port of call. After this will come teachers, work colleagues, those who knew you as a teammate or a band member, or so on. If it is a biography, then tell everyone you know what you are working on. You will probably find that nearly all of them will have contacts of their own or suggestions for where you should go for information. Some of these – perhaps the majority – will not be relevant but many will be good ideas that will save you much valuable time.

You may even find others working in a similar field who have contacts and information that they are willing to share. Certainly, someone who has done something similar recently will have much useful advice to impart. Someone who has, say, written a biography of their father who was a submariner during the Second World War will have lots to say about how to go about finding the relevant records of your own great-grandfather if he was a sailor during the First World War.

ONLINE SOURCES

Most people these days begin any research with the Internet. And it is true that search engines have brought a staggering amount of research about almost anything within reach of everyone. And most of it's free, too. The trouble is that a lot of it is rubbish. There's no filter, no quality control. Anyone can say anything they like about anything at all and publish it as fact. Lunatics and fanatics, freaks and weirdoes of every shape haunt the alleyways of the Internet like a particularly ferocious breed of zombie in a horror flick. There's a lot of seductive nonsense out there and you'll need patience and a highly developed nose for nonsense to avoid being infected by it. Tread carefully and trust nothing on the web unless it comes from unimpeachable sources.

It is, however, getting better. Just as the Wild West was cleaned up as the banks and railroads moved into the lawless frontier towns, so the virtual cities of the web are becoming more orderly. Many of the major libraries – including those of most universities – now have a web presence and you can access their resources from your living room. Likewise, one of your major research tools – the *Dictionary of National Biography* – can be studied via the Internet.

In the UK, census returns up to 1911 are also available on the Internet now, as are many other government records. Churches too – which were for a long time the principal record keepers – have begun to place some of their records online.

Here is a list of some of the websites that you might find most useful in your research:

A2A – the Access to Archives project – www.a2a.org.uk

This contains catalogues of numerous archives in England and Wales.

SCAN – the Scottish Archives Network – www.scan.org.uk

This aims to provide a single electronic catalogue of the records held in more than 50 Scottish archives. SCAN also aims to make some documents, for example the wills and testaments of Scots from 1500 to 1875, available online.

NRA – the National Register of Archives – www.hmc.gov.uk.nra

The NRA is maintained by the Historical Manuscripts Commission and allows searches of a wide range of archives. It covers archive deposits across the UK as well as listing UK material in foreign archives.

The Church of the Latter Day Saints (Mormons) – www.familysearch.org

The Mormons place enormous emphasis on genealogy and so they have launched a massive project to transcribe all the birth, death and marriage records from around the world. The Church also maintains a number of Family History Centres providing facilities where researchers can study.

1911 Census (England and Wales) – www.1911census.co.uk

This has much useful information for those researching the past. Go to www.nationalarchives.gov.uk/records/census-records.htm for information on censuses in England and Wales prior to this date, and www.scotlandspeople.gov.uk/ for censuses in Scotland.

LIBRARIES AND PUBLIC RECORDS OFFICES

There is no better index to how civilized a society has become than the way it funds and values its libraries. These quiet places devoted to study and to reading are free and open to everyone. Many schools and colleges have recently done away with the notion of a library. They have decided that they aren't cool, that kids are put off using them because of their intimidating name. They rename the space the LRC – short for Learning Resource Centre. This prompts the cynical response that maybe we should rename books themselves. Maybe we should call them HLDs – Handheld Learning Devices. This kind of Newspeak is nonsense, of course. A library *is* a learning resource centre. That's what the word means and so now, in its ridiculous efforts to be 'with it' and 'trendy', the school uses three words instead of one. The place itself hasn't changed. It's still a roomful of books plus some computers. And nearly all libraries are fitted out with PCs now. There's nothing special about that.

But the best thing about libraries is the librarians. Librarians are generally hugely knowledgeable about all manner of subjects, and making friends with the librarian at your local library means that you will save yourself an enormous amount of time. Every query that you have, big or small, is almost certainly one that they'll have heard and dealt with already. The same is true of public records offices. There is nothing like being led gently through a maze of ancient documentation by someone who knows all the pathways and safe routes out.

Focus point

If you are serious about researching the past, then becoming a regular face at your nearest library is one of the most useful and important things you can do. This is equally true of your nearest public records office. If they are any good, the staff who work in these places will be delighted to hear about your projects and to spend time dealing with your questions. It's what they do. It is what they are for.

USEFUL TOOLS

There are many useful tools to be found in libraries and archives and the following list should give you some sense of how important it is for the creative non-fiction writer to know their way around these places.

Here are some of the most typical forms of material that you will find in a local archive or library that might be most helpful to you:

Voters' rolls or register of electors

These provide evidence for residence and evidence of socio-economic status. Remember that women didn't get the vote until 1918 (and then it was only for those over 30) and it wasn't until 1928 that they gained full equality with men (votes for all at age 21). Single women got the vote in municipal elections in 1869. The franchise was also restricted for men prior to 1867.

Valuation rolls

These are very useful for establishing property ownership and for deducing from this the social status of an occupant.

School records

School logbooks can reveal a great deal about life outside the classroom, the impact of local epidemics being just one example. More obviously, admission registers, reports and school logbooks can provide specific information about a crucial aspect of your subject's childhood development.

Welfare records

Included in these records might be the records and logs of workhouses and other forms of relief paid to those who were destitute or unable, through illness or old age, to provide for themselves or their families.

Local authority records

These might include the minutes of local authority meetings, as well as documents relating to local planning, health, welfare, education, streets, shops, pavements and so on. Local authorities also maintained the burgess rolls, which are very valuable documents for discovering information on people during times of very limited franchise. (Burgesses are, broadly, heads of households with property and a trade, and therefore they often had the right to vote.)

Church records

These include information not only on births, marriages and deaths but also on education and welfare. In addition, many people were employed by the Church, and records and accounts can provide valuable information about life in the parish.

Local newspapers

Libraries may well have complete back issues of newspapers (including many that no longer exist) and you may find your subject appearing in the pages of their local paper, either in news reports, in the letters columns or as the subject of an obituary.

Local directories

These usually consist of an alphabetical listing of property owners and tenants and quite often give the occupations of the householders, too. In addition to this information, they frequently give details on justices of the peace, local societies and charities, and voluntary bodies.

Organizing your material

The temptation, when you are relying on research, is to stick in everything you know about a subject. You will have discovered amazing facts, and a lot of them, and it is natural to want to give as complete a picture as possible. That is, however, not your job. Your job is to make the subject come alive and you can't do that by including everything. You have got to tell a story and to do that you have to work on shaping your material. Just as a sculptor discards most of the clay or bronze he is working with, so much of your information is not going to make it into the main body of your book. The key is to read, summarize and select.

Keeping it legal

The three basic things to be aware of in keeping a non-fiction book on the right side of the law are:

- copyright
- permissions
- acknowledgements.

Copyright exists to protect authors from having their work stolen. If you quote short extracts – a line or two – for educational purposes, then this is usually all right. If you want to quote longer chunks of another writer's work, you will need to get the permission of the copyright holder and there will usually be a fee involved in this. If the writer is dead, copyright on their works will be held by their estate and is usually retained for 70 years after their death. (There are exceptions, and different laws apply in different countries, so do check.)

Copyright exists on letters and legal documents as well as on books and published material, so you will have to gain permission from the owners of these rights, too, if you wish to quote from them. It is the writer of the letter who owns the copyright – *not* the receiver. So even if you are the recipient of a hundred letters from a great-aunt vividly detailing her experiences as a spy during the Second World War, you can't publish extracts from them without getting express permission – in writing – from her or her estate.

Official documents such as birth and marriage certificates are also subject to copyright. In the UK, this is generally owned by the Crown or the Local Authorities. Again, permission must be sought – and usually paid for – before publication.

 ## Credit your sources

Copyright can be a fraught, vexing and tiresome business but it is absolutely essential that you make sure you are covered. It should also go without saying that all material you use should be acknowledged. All sources should be properly credited from the books you have used, all the way to that ten-minute interview you did with Uncle Herb in his retirement home on the Costa Brava.

Writing a proposal

We'll cover more about getting books published in a later chapter, but there are some clear differences between the paths to publication for non-fiction books and for novels that are worth dealing with here.

Unlike novels, non-fiction books are usually sold to publishers on the basis of a proposal and a sample chapter. Most agents and publishers are not – at an early stage with an untried author – going to read a whole manuscript. You need to put together a persuasive proposal. This proposal needs to be short and punchy. But it needs to get across some important information. It needs to tell the editor what your qualifications are for telling this story, so any expertise or experience that you have needs to be flagged up. It also needs to give the publishers or agents some idea of the potential market for the book.

Editors are, quite rightly, interested in projects that will make them money and you need to be aware of this, too. You'll need to indicate what other books on this subject exist and what your book will add. If no books exist, then that is worth pointing out. Explain clearly who or what the subject of the book is and why he, she or it is worth writing about.

Communicate your passion

Spend some real time on your proposal. It needs to give the flavour of the piece, so your distinctive voice needs to come over clearly. You are aiming to intrigue and excite, so style is important. The storytelling skills of a non-fiction writer are important. You know that the story you have to tell is fascinating and alive; it demands to be heard. You must communicate that passion to an editor in your sample chapter.

Submitting will be covered in more detail in Chapter 15 but, just in case you rush ahead without reading the rest of the book, remember that your text should be neatly and correctly printed out, double-spaced on one side and not bound or stapled. Do remember to number your pages and have your contact details on your covering letter. You'll find out more about covering letters later on.

Write a proposal

Write a two-page proposal for a non-fiction subject that you think might interest an editor. It can be for an autobiography, a biography or any other subject. Remember, your aim is simply to intrigue your reader enough that they ask to see more of your work.

This fairly long chapter reflects the fact that creative non-fiction is a growing area of interest among writers, readers and publishers. The final exercise in this chapter is adapted from one by the biographers Carole Angier and Sally Cline who, between them, have written ten major biographies including those on Zelda Fitzgerald, Primo Levi and Radclyffe Hall. It is good for showing the differences between biographical and autobiographical writing. It also shows how much you can accomplish in a short amount of time.

Write a biographical piece

You'll need a partner for this.

1. Interview a friend or a family member (or, even better, another writer) about an event or a relationship in their past. Keep it short; 15 minutes should be plenty of time if you can keep them focused.

2. Write a biographical piece based on the interview. Take no more than 30 minutes to write the piece.

3. Ask your subject to comment on the piece.

The above exercise is actually quite sophisticated, so, if it doesn't work out the first time, find a new subject and try it again. It's a particularly good one to try with someone else who wants to write because then you can experience what it is like to be the interviewee. This is an extremely useful thing to have done when you come to interview people for real.

 Ian Marchant

'If someone came to me saying, "I've a great idea for a non-fiction book," I'd say, "Excellent, but the idea has to be the easy bit, so think of another two good ideas before you over-commit to the first one." Ideas can't be copyrighted; they are just out there. Sometimes what might seem like a great idea for you might well have occurred to at least one other writer. Keep the ideas coming. Write a 200-word summation of the three ideas, then chew on 'em for a bit. Only when you're really happy with your original idea, and have weighed it against other possibilities, should you begin to write your book proposal.

'And I'd also like to tell this anecdote: I once took an idea for a radio travel programme to the BBC. The producer listened to my idea and then said, "Why you and not someone famous?"

I didn't have an answer at the time, but now I know that the ideas I pitch could only be done by me. Make sure that your book can only be written by you.'

(Ian Marchant is the author of the memoirs The Longest Crawl *and* Parallel Lines *(both Bloomsbury).)*

Where to next?

We've seen the wealth of subject matter available to the creative non-fiction writer and looked at ways to improve your research skills. In the next chapter we'll be looking at another kind of creative non-fiction, this time a little further from home – travel writing.

6

Travel writing

All writers, travel writers in particular, need the ability to look hard at the everyday. Readers of travel articles and books are looking for the writer to give them a flavour of the spirit of a place, and, paradoxical as it might seem, you can only do this by writing in detail about it. You can't resort to waffle. If your readers are thinking that one day they too might want to go to the same place, you will need to give them practical tips to help them find their way around, facts about the country to enable them to travel safely and with as little inconvenience as possible.

In this chapter you will learn about the importance of paying attention to your surroundings and how to make the familiar exotic. You'll find out what readers want from travel writing and understand how to put yourself in the picture.

Stand and stare

The one necessity of any kind of writing is to pay attention to what is going on around us. Most people are too caught up in the business of living to take the time to properly stand and stare. In most walks of life, simply watching the world go by is frowned upon. Do too much of it and it can get you fired or divorced. We live in a time when people are expected to have full diaries: to juggle work, family and relationships around a tight and full schedule. Every unforgiving minute should be used to the full and squeezed for every second of potential.

 ## Benjamin Disraeli

'Like all great travellers, I have seen more than I remember, and remember more than I have seen.'

But for the creative artist, and for the writer especially, taking the time and trouble to simply observe what's going on around us is actually the entire point of our work. The job of the writer is to make the strange comprehensible and also, of course, to make whatever is familiar new and strange. If most people don't have time amid the hurly-burly of life to make sense of it, the writer has to do it for them. We stand and stare so that others don't have to. By our example, perhaps those too caught up in the frenetic business of twenty-first-century life will start to learn to live at a more sustainable pace. Perhaps they too will discover the joys of simply looking and thinking.

 ## Focus point

Make time to stop and look around you. Drink it all in.

Write the details

Go to one of your favourite places and try to take a good, long, close look at all the details that make it special. Imagine that you are seeing it for the first time. What you are trying to do is collect a list of all the details that, when put together, will make a precise evocation of the place. Don't forget to include people in your notes. Now write a short piece describing the place in a way that might tempt people to visit.

Now rewrite

Now try to imagine why someone might dislike this place that you love so much. Would there be details that would infuriate them, or make them sad? Rewrite your piece accordingly.

Focus point

Travellers have a time budget as well as a financial one and so will need enough information to enable them to spend time as well as cash wisely.

Putting personality into the picture

It is likely that most of your readers will not necessarily be looking to visit the location you are writing about any time soon. They are visiting it vicariously, via your words. You will need to provide them with authentic, sensuous detail. They will want more than just the facts, however colourful: they are going to want to feel that they are in the company of a stimulating personality. They will want to trust their guide to impart knowledge but they will also want to spend time with someone of warmth and good humour.

Your personal voice

It is just as important with this kind of writing that your personal voice comes across, that your engagement with the culture you are describing is obvious.

The following exercises are by the writer Miranda France, whose book about Spain, *Don Quixote's Delusions: Travels in Castilian Spain*, is an intoxicating mixture of reportage, history, memoir and literary criticism. They are excellent for helping us to develop the skills necessary for bringing an unknown place alive for readers.

A still life

Think of an object in your home that would seem mundane to an outsider but is precious to you. In two paragraphs, try to describe the object, and then unfold a story behind it.

Sense of place

Dredge up the memory of a place you have been to. It could be somewhere you knew well and went to every day, or somewhere you have been to just once, say last night. Think about the smell and the sound of the place. If it was a chip shop, was the Formica sticky? What was on the radio? Was the smell agreeable or acrid? What were people talking about at the next table?

A desire

Write about a person or a thing you yearn for – it could be the love of your life or a cream cake. Make it deeply personal and poignant or utterly trivial and comic – or mix all of these elements.

All the best travel writers, from Daniel Defoe and Samuel Johnson in the eighteenth century through to the best modern travel writers such as Bill Bryson, Ian Marchant and Miranda herself, have all given a lot of themselves in their writing. It is the mixture of their acute and accurate observations and their personal style, plus the way that they drip-feed their own histories, that makes their take on places so appealing.

Paying attention

In order to write an interesting travel piece you don't need to go to exotic locations. You simply need the ability to look at the world in a new way and that means that you need to spend time just paying close attention to what happens around you all the time, wherever you happen to be.

Tom Miller

'Great travel writing consists of equal parts curiosity, vulnerability and vocabulary.'

Write a short piece

Write a piece about your home town or village designed to intrigue anyone who might not have visited it before. Try to make it as personal as you can but don't use more than 300 words.

Inevitably, some of you will live in beautiful places and others in areas considered drab by outsiders. I'd be willing to bet that pieces produced by those living in the less obviously attractive places are every bit as fascinating as pieces coming from those who live in beauty spots.

Workshop exercise

Now let's look at the piece of writing you've just produced in a bit more detail. Here are some questions for you to work through as you think about developing your work further.

1. Does your piece engage the senses? Can the reader not only 'see' your home town but hear it, even smell it?

2. It can be strangely thrilling to read a piece of writing set in the place where you're from. Are there any 'insider' references you can add as a nod to any locals reading your piece? Local characters, landmarks, legends? You don't want to exclude other readers, so make sure you explain your references to them, too.

3. People like to learn as they read, so try including interesting facts as well as descriptions. Did any events of historical importance happen there? Did any of the residents go on to become famous? Are there any local mysteries or unsolved crimes? Get online or visit the library and do some research. You might find out some things you never knew before.

4. Call someone else who lives in your town and ask them for their opinions on the place. Remember, one man's paradise is another man's purgatory. It's always good to get another perspective.

It's all about the people

All good writing is about people, in the final analysis. And people, wherever they live, are endlessly fascinating.

Christopher George

'Take boring notes. Menu prices, hotel tariffs, bus timetables, etc. There's no point describing a shikara's wake of burnished gold in the sunset-surface of Nageen Lake unless you can also tell me how much it costs to hire one. Evoke and inform, that's the mantra ... inform and evoke.'

(Christopher George is the author of Towards the Sun *(Hodder Murray).)*

Where to next?

In this chapter we've seen how important it can be to take time to just stand and stare, and been reminded that what is close to home can be just as interesting as the far-flung and exotic. However, if you are planning to travel, blogging can be a great way to chronicle your adventures. We'll be looking at blogging in the next chapter.

7

Blogging

Blogging is a way of reaching millions, possibly billions, of people with your thoughts and opinions. It is a public forum for discussion largely uncontrolled by governments, business and other self-appointed guardians of free speech. It is, or can be, a place where your voice can have as much weight as the most highly regarded writer.

The word 'blog' derives from 'web-log' and essentially means a diary. But, unlike the traditional diary where the writer keeps a secret record of their daily life, thoughts or feelings, the blogger makes the journal available to everyone online.

In this chapter you will learn what makes a successful blog and how to stand out in the 'blogocracy'. You will also find out about the many uses of blogging as a way of reaching your audience, as well as the dangers of blogging.

The magic of blogging

Blogging is, in theory at least, a return to the ferment of ideas that flourished in Europe just after the invention of the printing press. It is a defiantly democratic medium with the potential to empower ordinary people to express themselves without the filter of the traditional printed media with their phalanxes of editors standing between them and an audience. With blogging, you need no permission or commission to speak your mind. And you don't even have to expose yourself. You can do it anonymously. You can write about anything: from how delightful your grandchildren are to the evil of your government's foreign policy – sometimes within the same piece. You can post photos and music and videos.

Arthur C. Clarke

'Any sufficiently advanced technology is indistinguishable from magic.'

Blogging is a hugely powerful tool for building grassroots social movements, allowing activists to communicate their ideas directly to the people. On the other hand, it is also an opportunity for every eccentric with access to a laptop to pollute hyperspace with drivel of the most pernicious kind.

Of course the identity of the blogger may be secret – most people write under a pseudonym – but their activities and thoughts are very public. Blogging has had a powerful effect on the media life of this country. It has revolutionized the process of commenting on events.

We can all have a say

Via a blogging site anyone at all can have their say about almost anything. It is a valuable democratic tool and allows us insight into areas of life to which in past decades only the privileged few had access.

Who blogs?

Policemen blog. Nurses blog. Teachers blog. Doctors blog. MPs blog. Prostitutes blog. People under siege in war zones blog. So do the soldiers doing the besieging. Thanks to blogging sites, we have access to the thoughts of millions of ordinary people living all over the world. As a reader of blogs, you can read and respond to the daily record of life in all parts of the world and under all conditions.

Some of these blogs have become very famous. Belle de Jour is the pseudonym of a high-class call girl who writes a blog that became a very successful book and then a television drama in the UK starring Billie Piper. Newspapers scour the blogs to find out what ordinary people think about the news and adapt their content to suit. Meanwhile, publishers are always looking for a blog that might make a saleable book.

Why blog?

Part of the answer is contained in the paragraphs above. Blogging is a chance to say what you feel about current events, big and small. It is a chance to get your writing read by a global audience. It can even be a route to publication for a lucky, particularly interesting few. But its best benefit for an aspiring writer is that it encourages a habit of daily reflection.

Most writing teachers have always encouraged new writers to keep a diary as it helps your style enormously to keep a coherent record of your life. It gives invaluable practice in ordering your thoughts. And, of course, it is a record of events that you can work on later and hone into more polished pieces. A diary can build up into a treasure chest of future material.

Blogging is similar, with the added benefit that people can comment on your writing. They can, of course, comment unfavourably. And, more seriously, you might find other writers using your material. I know several professional writers who trawl blogs looking for inside info on occupations and lifestyles that might help with whatever they are writing about.

The technicalities

It can be astonishingly easy to set up a blog. You choose your hosting site, sign up with your email address and you're just a few clicks away from publishing your first post. You don't need any special technical know-how and there are plenty of online tutorials if you get stuck.

BLOGGING PLATFORMS

A blogging platform is the website that hosts your blog. Let's have a look at some of the most popular ones.

WordPress is a blogging behemoth. It offers two services:

- WordPress.com, which hosts your blog for you, for free, but allows you to choose from a vast selection of themes that will determine how your blog looks.
- WordPress.org, which lets you host your own blog. WordPress.org gives you complete freedom over your blog, but you do need some technical skills and it might not be the best option for a beginner with no knowledge of HTML coding or similar dark arts.

Blogger is Google's blogging platform. It's free, easy to use and you only need a Google/Gmail account to get started. The 'back end' of a Blogger blog – the place where you post and edit content – is relatively simple, which makes this site popular among beginner bloggers. It's easy to monetize a Blogger blog by allowing advertising, so, if you're very lucky, you might earn yourself enough for the occasional cup of tea.

Tumblr is a blogging-platform-meets-social-network that makes it really easy to share pictures, videos and text and to 'reblog' other people's posts. It's quick and simple to set up; it looks good and you can customize all aspects of your blog. Many people use Tumblr as a kind of online scrapbook, to curate their own archive of interesting content. Tumblr is very popular among the under-25s.

There are other blog hosting sites online, including those that require a fee. There's also the possibility of creating your own website, but that's something I have neither the space nor the technical know-how to help you with here.

Twitter

Twitter is a vastly popular microblogging site. A 'tweet' is a tiny blog post, no longer than 140 characters. This enforced brevity makes Twitter great for pithy observations and one-liners, which might be why it's so popular with writers and comedians. In fact, some writers have gone as far as to write entire novels on Twitter, with each mini-chapter comprising fewer than 140 characters.

WRITERS ON TWITTER

Here are just a handful of the writers you can follow on Twitter:

- Margaret Atwood (@margaretatwood)
- Ian Rankin (@beathigh)
- Stephen Fry (@stephenfry)
- Alexander McCall Smith (@McCallSmith)
- Chuck Palahniuk (@chuckpalahniuk)
- Jackie Collins (@Jackiecollins)
- Jodi Picoult (@jodipicoult)
- Anne Rice (@AnneRiceAuthor)

- Neil Gaiman (@neilhimself)
- Joanne Harris (@joannechocolat)
- Caitlin Moran (@caitlinmoran)
- Joyce Carol Oates (JoyceCarolOates)

Twitter is packed with useful resources for both writers and readers. Some other interesting accounts to follow are:

- Writers' Digest – @writersdigest
- McSweeney's (publisher and literary magazine) – @mcsweeneys
- Guardian Books – @guardianbooks
- Telegraph Books – @telegraphbooks
- New York Times Books – @nytimesbooks
- The London Review of Books – @lrb
- Galley Cat (information about the publishing industry) – @galleycat
- Writing Tips – @writing_tips

HASHTAGS

A hashtag is a word or phrase with a # symbol at the beginning. It's a way of tagging your tweet using key words so that others can find it. For example, if you wanted to see who was tweeting about the tennis, you could search Twitter for #wimbledon and you'd be able to see what other users were saying. Some interesting hashtags for writers include #writetips, #writing and #amwriting.

Warning

Twitter can be an excellent place for writers to find inspiration, advice and a community of like-minded people. Be careful though – it can be quite addictive and you don't want tweeting to eat into your writing time.

Use Twitter in a story

Pick a character from a story you've been working on and imagine that they have a Twitter account. Try to write a series of tweets from the perspective of your character as they experience the events of your story.

How to stand out from the crowd

If you have gone to the trouble of posting your thoughts up on the web, then you probably want at least a few readers. Yet with so many blogs, and with so few of any merit, why should readers wade through the many screen miles of turgid and self-regarding prose to discover your site?

The first thing is to make sure that what you have to say is going to be of real interest. It is time, therefore, to evaluate your life in terms of what might intrigue other people. Unlikely contrasts are always a good source of interest. Are you a middle-class, southern woman living on a big northern council estate? Are you a man doing what is usually considered to be a woman's job? Are you an older person sharing a university apartment with students many years younger than yourself? Do you have 11 children? Did you become a grandparent in your thirties? Do you live in an unusual place in an unusual set-up: a commune, for example, or a kibbutz? Did you quit a high-flying job to become a speech therapist?

Review your list

In Chapter 2 you wrote a huge list of all the places where you've worked and the interests you have. Go back to that list and highlight anything you think might make an interesting blog post.

SURPRISING TRUTHS

A game that is quite often played by those trying to bond groups of disparate individuals together is to get each member of the group to tell the others something about themselves that they think will surprise all the others. When playing this game I've had confessions ranging from the innocuous 'I've always wanted to run a pub', to the shyly boastful 'My band once appeared on *Top of the Pops*', to the compelling – if scary – 'I could kill you all with my bare hands.' (This last confession came from a mild-mannered lady on a children's writing course who, it turned out, had once been an officer in the British Special Forces.)

If you are going to blog, it makes sense to play this game on your own. What is there about your life that will surprise and intrigue the world? There is bound to be something. This is your chance to review what there is about your life that would be of immediate interest to a stranger. It is your 'unique selling point', or USP.

When you have decided, focus on that one thing. Try not to make your blog a sprawling repository of your thoughts and feelings on every subject. The key difference between a blog and a traditional diary is that you are writing for an audience.

You must engage your readers, keep them interested, so that they don't click to another part of the web. It's a hard trick to pull off. People browsing the web are like particularly restless jackdaws, forever wondering if there is a shinier nugget somewhere else in hyperspace.

Find your USP

Blogs work best when they document unusual perspectives.

Less is more

With the limited attention span of the web audience in mind, adhere firmly to the 'less is more' principle. Try to ration yourself to writing about just one thing that happens to you every day, or every week.

The decline of blogging?

There has been a lot of discussion online recently about the decline of blogging. Many of the avid bloggers of five years ago have found that they're flagging, finding it harder and harder to maintain the momentum necessary to keep their blogs fresh and up to date. Life gets in the way. Subjects exhaust themselves. Comments grow infrequent, new readers rare. With heavy hearts, bloggers admit defeat and slink offline, or, at the very least decamp, to Twitter.

It's true that a lot of the business once conducted in the comments sections of popular blogs is now taking place on Twitter and Facebook, and the first big wave of bloggers might well be receding, but that doesn't mean you shouldn't blog yourself. People do still read blogs, but busy lives both online and off mean that they have the time and inclination to read only the really good ones. If you have the content, they will come. In a strange way, blogs have become the books of the online world – the long-form works, the things you have to commit to and concentrate on, as opposed to the constant cacophony of tweets and 'likes' and status updates.

Some health warnings

Material you want to place on the web should be handled as though it were radioactive. After all, it might well lie there quietly polluting the future for longer than a piece of discarded uranium. Your thoughts, photos, videos, jokes and careless libels may be on the Net for ever, as incorruptible as disposable nappies in a landfill. And they are more public and more toxic!

Numerous talented potential leaders in all fields of human endeavour have had their achievements curtailed by a set of stupid photos taken at a drunken student party and then posted on the Internet, to be resurrected at the most cruelly inconvenient of moments. And it won't just be photos that cause trouble. If you write about your boss in terms that identify them, you could soon be looking for a new job.

One drawback of blogging is that people can very quickly become victims of their own success. Write a good one and word of mouth may quickly bring you a surprising number of regular readers, among whom may be people who think they know who you are. Some of them may be right.

The most famous diarist of them all was Samuel Pepys. His journals, written in shorthand, lay unread in a Cambridge University library for 150 years before being translated and published (and even then they were heavily edited). Imagine if Pepys had written a blog (maybe it would be www.confessionsofanavyofficeclerk.blogspot.com), his accounts of life in London would surely have garnered an audience very quickly. A junior civil servant nudges his mate in some open-plan office somewhere in Cheapside. The mate gets on to his girlfriend who works on a glossy lifestyle magazine. She writes a little piece about the racy double life led by public officials these days.

Pretty soon King Charles II is clicking on what we used to call the information superhighway to find a lavish description of Nell Gwynn's décolletage. He is not amused and thus one promising career in public service is ruined: Britain never gets her Navy sorted, and a hundred years later the French win the Napoleonic Wars.

Focus point

It might seem extreme, but words – and images – on the Net are never deleted and, even if you have completely forgotten their existence, they may come back to haunt you when you least expect it.

Blog about your life

Think about what you've done so far today. Select just one incident and write about that. If you can bring to your description some special insight into a part of your life that others don't know about, that will add something. Try to do this for the next week and show the results to a trusted friend (TF). If the TF likes what you've written and thinks both that it adds to the sum of human knowledge and won't get you (or anyone else you mentioned in it) into trouble in the foreseeable future, then – and only then – consider posting your blog.

Blogging in character

There's nothing to say that you have to blog as yourself. You can pretend to be anyone you like as long as you don't break any libel or copyright laws. You could write a blog for each character in a story you're working on and then have them comment on each other's posts. You could blog as a pirate, as the Tooth Fairy, as the monster who lives under your bed, as Cinderella, as anyone you can dream up.

Blog about a character

Choose a character from a piece you've been working on and write a series of blog posts documenting the events of the story. Then imagine that six months have passed and write another post showing how your character's life has changed.

Alternatively, pick a historical character, anyone you like, from Marie Antoinette to Jack the Ripper. Now write a blog post for them.

From blogs to books

There have been a number of high-profile cases of bloggers getting sizeable deals to turn their posts into books. Julie Powell's blog – about how her life as a dissatisfied office worker changed when she decided to try to cook all the recipes in Julia Child's *Mastering the Art of French Cooking* – became a successful book and then a film starring Meryl Streep.

Despite this and other successes, like the aforementioned Belle de Jour, you shouldn't go into blogging with one eye on a book deal. Yes, blogging about your novel and posting extracts from it can attract the attention of publishers and agents. Yes, your original and innovative blog idea might make a great stocking-filler book and could quite conceivably grace the till-side countertops of bookshops up and down the land, but don't put the cart before the horse. Some people go into blogging with elaborate battle-plans, determined to capitalize on any and all opportunities for publicity, and their sites end up as a shouty mess of self-promotion. You should concentrate first and foremost on making your blog the best *blog* it can be. A blog is an art form in itself and doesn't have to be just a means to an end.

Workshop exercise

In this exercise we'll reflect on everything we've learned in this chapter. Here is a series of questions to help you corral your ideas and create a great, popular blog.

1. What is your blog about? Can you sum it up in one sentence, for example 'My blog is about the difficulties and joys of raising a child with Asperger's Syndrome', 'My blog is about the confessions of a call-centre worker', 'My blog is about my quest to become a professional magician'?

2. Are there any other blogs out there in the ether that cover the same subject? There may well be, but that doesn't mean you don't have a unique perspective. You might even find that writers covering similar ground become part of your online community, maybe even a cyberspace friend.

3. Would you mind if your mum, your partner or your boss read your blog? It is possible to be anonymous on the Internet, but be very careful if you think your blog could get you into trouble.

4. Are you involved with the blogocracy? Comment on blogs you like and don't be afraid to ask questions. Contact other bloggers, ask them how they improve their traffic, how they maintain their momentum. The Internet is much friendlier than it's made out to be and most bloggers will be pleased to help.

5. Most importantly, is each post you write as good as it could possibly be? You can post a blog immediately, but that doesn't mean you should post it as soon as you've written it. Blog posts, just like poems, short stories, articles and the rest, should be subjected to a stringent editing process. Have you checked and double-checked your work? Has it done its time in the drawer? Have you read it out loud to yourself? Once it's up online, it's up, and although you can edit or delete your posts, you can't be sure who's already seen them.

Caroline Smailes

'I think that the key to blogging is the interactive element, being prepared to visit and comment and respond to comments given to you. Developing and being accepted into networks requires effort, like any developing friendship. Content and style vary and are a matter of personal taste. For me, the blogs that I enjoy have an honesty, a social interaction, a persona that is interesting and accessible.'

(Caroline Smailes' blog can be found at www.carolinesmailes. co.uk. Her novel In Search of Adam (The Friday Project) was published after she wrote about it on the web.)

Where to next?

Now that we've glimpsed the vastness of cyberspace and its potential as both a resource and a platform for writers, it's time to go offline, to unplug ourselves and venture outside, into the giddy playground that is writing for children.

8

Writing for children

Children need wholesome stories in the same way that they need fibre and fruit. Just as there has been a concerted effort in recent years to reintroduce children to the benefits of exercise and decent nutrition, there has been, similarly, with less media fanfare, a battle that many parents, publishers, librarians and teachers have been fighting to engage children once more with the joy of reading.

In this chapter you will learn why writing for children is so important and just what makes a great children's book. Writing for children is a challenge: children are very opinionated about the books they do like. You will also discover what you need to know when deciding what age group to write for, about the necessity of honesty and the joy of being rude, and how to deal with potential pitfalls.

The rarest kind of 'best'

Our children deserve the best and that is as true for writing as it is for anything else. We live in a culture of plenty. Most people in the industrialized world have plenty of food, decent accommodation, as well as education, health, recreation and entertainment facilities that would astonish our recent ancestors. Everyone in the UK and the US is already a lottery winner when compared with the majority of the world's population. And yet we often seem determined to squander these gifts. Many of our children are bored witless despite a plethora of entertainment choices that someone born even just a generation back can only marvel at.

As recently as the 1970s who could have predicted digital television, never mind the rise of the Internet games where hundreds of thousands of players compete without ever meeting – without even being on the same continent? We have Wii, PSP, Nintendo DS, giant plasma-screen HD televisions and computer games to suit every taste and yet … and yet … many children seem restless and dissatisfied and parents are consequently frustrated and cross. The trouble is that a lot of the entertainment choices pushed at children are junk, the equivalent of a non-stop diet of fizzy pop and sweets. A good book can show them that life needn't be lived through a lens.

Reading might seem hard work when compared with sitting in front of the television all day. And nearly every parent has used children's television as a babysitter from time to time. And yes, television and computers can be educational, but so can dissection and we don't usually allow children to undertake that kind of experiment unsupervised.

 Alfred Noyes

'Oh, grown-ups cannot understand
And grown-ups never will,
How short's the way to fairy land
Across the purple hill.'

The main drawback of allowing children unfettered access to the various screen-based entertainments is that the lassitude it induces becomes addictive. Did you know that watching television uses less energy than sleeping? But even worse than this is the fact that a room without someone burbling away in the corner begins to seem unnatural to children. They become unnerved by quiet and by reflection because it is so rare to them. They become scared of it, in the way that previous generations were scared of woods and the dark.

> ## Focus point
>
> The modern world is loud and bright and children have access to unlimited entertainments. Reading can offer a rare and vital moment of peace and reflection.

What is the real thing?

We all know that a book is the real thing for a child when that child demands to have it read to them again and again. A story is the real thing when we know every word by heart and still we want it read to us. A book is the real thing when it completely absorbs the child. Crucially, it also needs to engage adults. For younger children, a big part of the enjoyment of being read to is spending time on a shared activity with a grown-up. If it is clear that the grown-up in question is bored and would rather be doing something else, then the child will become anxious, distressed and restless too.

Children are a difficult audience. Not only do books have to compete with all the other entertainments in what has become a visual rather than a literary culture, but children demand to be engrossed. Generally, kids like books that are funny, that are full of adventure, that feature strong, close relationships, that are gripping without being too frightening and that end more or less happily. It's a tall order but, on the plus side, if a child loves your book then they will love it for ever, read it over and over, and seek out other stories that you may write.

Remember your favourites

Write a list of your favourite books from childhood. Without revisiting them, write what you can remember of the storyline. Now write down why you loved those books and what they taught you. Next time you're in the library, try to read them again. Do they still have that magic?

Your audience

Children are a loyal and passionate audience as well as a demanding one. They are honest, too. If a small girl says she loves your book, you know that she's not just being nice; she really does love it. If a lad says your book is 'well ace', then you have a real fan. Adults will say things just to be nice whereas kids, however polite, will give it to you straight.

We once had a poet teach a course at the writing centre who asked a group of Liverpool schoolchildren what they thought of the poem he had just read them. There was a half-second pause before a girl piped up, 'I thought it were rubbish. Really borin", whereupon the poet took offence. Thankfully, the opposite story is more usual, where children meet an author and find that they are pleasantly surprised by how enthralled they have become just by having someone read something to them. The thrill of being gradually drawn into a story can appear like a kind of low-key miracle to many of today's children.

Deciding on an age group

This is your first challenge when writing for children but it is worth thinking about right at the beginning. What is also worth getting right early on is how children at a particular age think and speak today. An eight-year-old in the twenty-first century may well not talk or even think as an eight-year-old did in 1972. Even though the fundamentals probably haven't changed all that much, the language and culture that surrounds today's eight-year-old is very different. It obviously helps to know some children!

Whatever age you decide to write for, the crucial thing is not to patronize or talk down to your audience. Children want to be talked to on the level. As any schoolteacher will tell you, in conversation with a child it is always best to assume that they are a little older, a little more well-read and a little more articulate than they actually are.

Don't patronize

Children like to be thought of as grown up and will rise to the occasion if treated in this way. It's no different with books. Write plainly and simply, but don't write childishly.

Madeleine L'Engle

'You have to write the book that wants to be written. And if the book will be too difficult for grown-ups, then you write it for children.'

Look at the categories

When you next visit a bookshop, spend some time in the children's section. Take notice of how the books are arranged. Generally, publishers and booksellers want to put your book into a category. Is it a baby book, a book for pre-schoolers or a picture book for children between five and seven years old? Or is it 'core fiction', that is, for seven to twelve-year-olds? Above that age you are writing for 'young adults'. Spend some serious time browsing and reading, rediscovering your own preferences. What categories are you most drawn to?

If you are uncertain where your own style might fit, try writing a paragraph or two of a story for each age group. Have some books to hand to help with vocabulary and style.

Spend time with some children. Get them to bring you their favourite books. Read to them, or get them to read to you if they're old enough. Play some games with them, but remember to let them take the lead. The children will be delighted. It's no easy task for even the most winning child to get an adult's close attention. It helps if you've got your own to hand, but grandchildren, nieces, nephews, the kids next door or those at the local school will also appreciate you taking an interest. (If you're going into a school, you will need to get proper permission and apply for a DBS check, which the school can arrange.)

Losing past loves

One of the great things about writing for children is that the books young people fall in love with stay a treasured memory for ever. Like childhood itself, a book can often seem even better when seen through the enchanted specs of memory. You will have your own favourite stories and characters: there's a good chance that you may well have been passionately attached to the Famous Five, the Fantastic Four, Just William, Swallows and Amazons, Molesworth, Biggles, Tracy Beaker, Narnia, The Borrowers or Harry Potter.

As a writer, you need to let them go. Remember what you liked about them, certainly, but don't think that they will come to your aid now. The world is a very different place and children, being infinitely adaptable, are wired for the one they find themselves in.

Focus point

Read as much modern children's literature as you can.

Update a classic

Try to find a passage in a classic children's book that you particularly enjoy and rewrite it in a style that a modern child might appreciate, updating the language and setting as you see fit. Be careful. It's harder than you think to update an acknowledged classic and still make it inspiring and rich.

Originality

Having an original idea that has the legs to sustain an entire book is perhaps the hardest thing in all writing. You might find yourself coming close to despair. All the best ideas for children's fiction can seem as if they're already taken. In particular, stories involving toys that come to life, animals with human characteristics, and trainee wizards all seem to have been done to death. Nevertheless, themes for children's books are universal and timeless – the secret world, the magical journey, unexpected dangers, being lost, gaining new powers – and original ways of treating these themes are all around you just waiting to be discovered.

In essence, all children's stories, from baby books to the most hard-edged, realistic teen fiction, are all about making sense of, and expressing wonder at, a big and sometimes frightening world. If you want to write fiction for children, then you need to look at the world as if you were a child as well as a writer. Having access to your childhood self is useful for all writers – Graham Greene described childhood as a writer's capital – but for a writer of young people's fiction it is absolutely essential.

Go small

Try taking your notebook to a public place – a library is a safe bet but you could try it in a shopping mall or a sports centre – and make yourself physically small. Sit on the floor and make detailed notes about how it feels to be looking up at everything and everyone.

Giving power to the weak

It's possible to say that there is an element of empowering the underdog in all great children's literature. It is unsurprising that children respond particularly well to stories where the weak emerge victorious. However loved and cared for, a child is always living under a dictatorship. The range of decisions they can make is limited. Their power is small compared with that of the adults around them. Literature for children should be subversive – a kind of protest song. Children in books should make important life-changing decisions; they should have special powers, whether these are supernatural or merely those that result from a keen wit. In other words, children should be at the centre of the world you create. Your universe should be a child's universe.

Of course, some of you will be planning worlds where animals are at the centre, or toys or creatures entirely of your own devising. And this is fine – not only fine, but great. However, it is still the case that it's the smaller animals, the tiniest creatures, that should come out on top in the end.

Focus point

Your heroes must always, always win. And your villains (probably adults) should suffer in inventive ways. Take Roald Dahl as a guide. Part of Dahl's appeal was not only that he knew that people – including children – could be spiteful, cruel and idiotic, but also that he was prepared to exaggerate these traits for the entertainment of his audience. And spite, cruelty and idiocy always prove the undoing of his villains.

Get your revenge

You'll love this. Make a list of all the people who have ever done you wrong. Now, next to their name, try to think of something that should happen to them. Make it comical if you can. Make it gory, grim and gruesome if you like. Try to make the punishment fit the crime. Revenge is a perfectly acceptable motive in all drama and children are very keen on justice. Aim for at least ten 'incidents' and you'll have enough material for several children's stories.

The joy of rudeness

Underpants are always funny. We know this. So are bottoms. Children are innocently tickled by the things that seem to embarrass adults: aliens that steal underpants, dinosaurs that eat them, people who wear them on their heads. Surreal uses of the everyday and the vulgar will score points with the smaller crowd. Don't be afraid to fart, belch and have stomachs rumble at serious volume.

Your guts for garters

'I'll have your guts for garters' was a favourite phrase of my grandmother's. I didn't understand it, but it sounded deliciously frightening. This is exactly the effect that you might want to create in your audience. Children absolutely love blood and gore. Adults don't, however (or those reading to young children don't, anyway). And they are at least half your audience.

As a responsible writer of children's fiction you should make sure that any violence in your books is there for a reason, that it helps the story along. Yes, of course we want to frighten our audience a bit. Yes, we want to make them shiver. But we want them to enjoy the thrill of the rollercoaster we're giving them. We don't want them to feel sick and want to get off. Whether you are Virginia Woolf or Dr Seuss, all writing is about getting readers to turn the page, hungry to find out what happens next. You don't want to terrify young readers.

Make fear fun

Think back to the most frightening moment you had as a child. Write it down as plainly and as simply as you can. Now write it down in a way that makes light of the situation somehow. Try writing it as a cartoon, or in rhyme. Or introduce something mad like a purple elephant floating into the story in a hot-air balloon. The aim here is to surprise yourself as much as any younger readers.

Extreme characters

Extreme characters are fun to write and children's fiction would seem to be a natural home for them – especially extremely nasty characters. Again, Roald Dahl is a good example of a writer who is unconstrained by the need to find redeeming features in his characters. In adult fiction, people find it difficult to believe in someone who is wholly bad and even harder to enthuse about someone who is wholly good. Our heroes these days must be tainted by flaws, which they endeavour to resolve by the end of the book, while our villains often have a reason for their moral turpitude. This isn't necessarily so with characters in children's books and this can be hugely liberating.

As was said right at the beginning of this book, writing should be playing and it should be fun. Essentially, it is 'What if ...' and 'Let's pretend ...' and producing larger-than-life characters is part of the joy of fiction for children. Everything can be bigger, brighter, more black and white than would be acceptable in the greyer, more psychologically accurate world of writing for adults.

The problem of problems

Part of the point of reading is to make sense of the world we are in, to try out different ways of being. This is especially important for children who are travelling without maps a lot of the time. When a problem comes up in our lives there is a good chance that we adults have a storehouse of solutions to draw on. If not, we know that there will be places and people we can go to who have the requisite experience. Children often have only the choice of blind faith in peers, family or teachers, or trying to work things out on their own. It's a difficult world and being a child is not for the timid. There are real and emotional dangers at every turn. And books, like the best films and the best television, or like a conversation with a good friend, can present children with dilemmas and choices in a safe way. Identifying with the struggles of a character in a book (even if that character is a lonely pig or a homesick dinosaur) can also be a valuable way for a child to develop empathy and emotional literacy.

Don't preach

Children also hate being lectured. They get enough of being told what to do, so they are going to be naturally resistant to being told what to think. Stories where it is obvious that there is a didactic intent are likely to be little loved by children, however laudable their aims. It is hard for an author to create a character that engages if that character owes their place on the page to the need to teach the readers a lesson. Children sometimes love their teachers, but they rarely love a teacher's pet. And the characters that are in the book to show us exactly how we should or shouldn't behave are going to be the worst kinds of characters. They are going to be wooden and lifeless. And we won't trust them.

I began my working life teaching drama to troubled children and it seemed that every week we were being encouraged to set up anti-bullying workshops where children would be asked to devise stories around bullying that ended happily. All the children I ever taught could dream up any number of scenarios where a bully was eventually defeated by the actions of defiant kids acting in concert with their noble teachers, but it didn't seem to make much difference to the actual incidence of bullying. The workshops had simply become another lesson with a 'right answer' that had to be given in order to keep 'Sir' happy. Good children's books are driven by conflict and problem solving but they need surprise, and too many issue-based books lack this essential element.

A good way to make sure that the problems your characters overcome are real is to make sure that the problems arise naturally from their characters. In other words, create the characters in detail so that you know them intimately (this is just as important if your characters are rabbits or moles or rats or any other creature real or imagined – or mythological for that matter!), and the themes, issues and how they deal with them will then come out in an organic, unforced way.

Write characters

Try to think of a moral or a message that you consider important for children to learn. Now come up with a short storyline (keep it to just one page of A4) that illustrates this, involving two or more characters. Now write detailed character descriptions of those characters. Write down absolutely everything you can think of. Make sure you get in all their likes and dislikes. Now revisit your storyline and inhabit it with the fully rounded characters. Remember the rule: *you* need to know everything about your character's history. When it comes to the story, however, the readers don't.

Illustrations

Unless you are a talented artist, don't bother doing the drawings for any of your stories yourself. Nor should you get a friend to illustrate them (unless your friend is genuinely gifted in this area). If your story comes to the notice of a publisher, they will probably want to choose an illustrator themselves, someone who fits with their house style and whom they are used to working with. They've already taken a big chance by accepting your work; it's asking a lot to get them to take on a new illustrator as well.

Poetry for children

Children love rhythm and rhyme. They also love alliteration, onomatopoeia, puns and wordplay of all kinds. Part of the joy of writing for children is that exuberant verse finds ready appreciation. Clever or outrageous rhymes and vivid imagery, as well as a gripping narrative, can greatly endear a book to a child. You don't want to make it too obvious, however. You want to pile surprise on surprise for your audience. In general, a good rule is to go for the third rhyme that you think of. The first is one that children might think of for themselves. The second is one that their parents will think of. The third rhyme that occurs to you may be the original, startling one that delights. It may also be the word that prompts you to take your story in directions that surprise even you, the writer.

Sharing stories

🔑 Your inner child

You are the most important element in the story. You don't need to be young to be a great writer of children's stories, but you do need to be able to stay connected to the child inside yourself. You need to identify with that girl who got left out of games at playtime, or the boy who fell off his bike. But it is your ideas and, most importantly, your passions and enthusiasms that will come off the page and engage younger readers.

Remember, children aren't the same as us. They are not cynical or distrustful. They expect to be liked and admired. They expect that people will find their stories fascinating and in return they expect that you are a nice, friendly entertaining person with a fund of stories of your own. And they are right. Spend time with children and you will want to make yourself worthy of their trust in you. And you will want your stories to be treasured, too, and you will work hard to make them as good as they can be because this audience really does deserve the best of you.

Workshop exercise

This workshop is actually going to involve other people, albeit small ones. Write a story for your chosen age group. Spend a lot of time on it, just as you would on a story for adults. Read it aloud to yourself. Put it away for a while and then redraft it. Then put it away again and redraft it again. Get a candid, constructive reader friend to make suggestions. Redraft it again. Now get a child of the right age group to read it. Make any more necessary changes.

Now comes the crucial test: read it to a small group of the right age group at a nearby school or youth group (having first got all the proper authorities to agree through all the right channels). Elicit their honest reactions and solicit suggestions for how it could be improved. As with any advice, you are free to ignore it. Some of it will no doubt be contradictory anyway, but what you can't ignore is the feeling in the room. That never lies.

You will be able to tell if your story is holding the attention of its target audience. However well behaved your audience is, if their concentration is faltering then a dozen tiny rustlings and fidgets and whisperings will let you know. Even if the kids are silent, there will be something about the dead quality of the air that will tell you which parts have failed to grab them. Similarly, the atmosphere will become subtly charged if your story is doing its job.

Here are some questions you might want to ask your audience, to guide them towards giving you some useful advice:

1. *Who was your favourite character?* They might say the hero of the piece but they are just as likely to choose the villain or the wisecracking dog. If one character proves particularly popular, consider making them the star of your next story.

2. *If you were a character in this story, what would you have done differently?* Children often tackle problems with lateral thinking beyond any adult. You may never have thought about defeating an alien invasion with ice cream, but a child might be able to tell you just how to go about it.

3. *What would you like to see the characters do next?* This is a shameless ask for ideas, but if you can take your most popular characters on new, exciting adventures, you may have a series on your hands.

4. *What didn't you like?* This is a good way to identify any boring bits in your story, and to learn what to avoid in the future.

5. *What did you learn from the story?* By asking this you'll find out whether the moral of your story was clear and whether the children will remember it.

Some of you will be better readers and performers than others. But it is surely part of a writer's job to be able to read their own work well. If you are not a natural performer, it really is worth putting the hours in and improving. It is something you can learn with practice and repetition.

Lee Weatherly

'To write for children you need to cast yourself back to your childhood self. It's not enough to observe children and then try to write about them from the outside in; you need to feel it yourself, from the inside out. Rediscover play; walk silently through the woods and wonder; ask 'What if?' Being a children's writer doesn't really have anything to do with having children; it's all about connecting with those feelings within yourself – and then writing them.'

(Lee Weatherly is the author of Child X (David Fickling Books).)

Where to next?

Over the previous chapters we've examined all kinds of writing. The exercises you've completed should have resulted in a notebook bulging with good ideas. Next, we're going to see how those ideas can be turned into one of the most demanding art forms of all – the novel.

9

Starting to write
a novel

You may not have begun working your way through this
book with the idea that you would become a novelist, but the
novel seems to be the ultimate dream of most writers. Of all
creative writing courses, those on novel writing are the most
in demand. This chapter explores the exciting challenge
novel writing offers you, and suggests ways to kick-start
your book. It looks at various aspects of novel writing
including how to decide on a central character and theme,
the importance of voice and the basics of structure.

If, after tackling the exercises in this chapter, you decide
you don't want to write novels, you have still completed an
important part of a writer's journey – that is, deciding what
kind of writer you are.

The challenge

It seems that even successful writers in other fields – playwrights, screenwriters, journalists and children's writers and bloggers – still often want to pit themselves against the challenge of writing a novel. Only some poets – and perhaps some short-story writers – seem immune to this siren call.

Writing a novel is a long and complicated process, and there simply isn't the space here to go into as much detail as the subject deserves. This chapter concentrates on the initial stages of writing a novel – generating ideas, deciding on characters, themes and voice – and in next chapter covers the more advanced stages of the journey, including dialogue, setting, planning and plot.

 ## John Updike

'A novel is nothing less than the subtlest instrument for self-examination and self-display that mankind has invented yet.'

If you decide you do want to become a novelist, I recommend you move on to *Write a Novel and Get It Published* (Teach Yourself, 2010), which will help you with every aspect of the novel-writing process.

The exploration begins

The territory

Every new novel is a vast and undiscovered continent. And every journey through that continent is a partnership between your conscious and the deeper, hidden parts of your psyche.

Your subconscious and your rational mind will move forward through this new territory together, often arguing about the roads to take. Your subconscious will want to drive to the darkest places, while your rational brain will want to take easier routes, cut down obstacles, build roads and generally impose order on chaos. Your unconscious is a pioneer and your conscious self is like a colonial administrator, attempting to impose carefully constructed systems on this difficult, lawless territory.

And there's the question of population, too. Of all the real-life continents a novel might resemble, the best example is probably Australia. When your novel begins to take shape it is a land that you, as an explorer, know nothing about. The first thing you notice is that it seems a wild place, but abundant, too, rich in possibilities. And then you'll start transporting a population into it. But on the journey to the new world, these characters have been growing; it seems they've got plans independent of whatever you've got in mind for them and, within moments of landing, some or all of your characters have escaped into the wilderness. Others, for whom you had high hopes, won't survive.

As you and your people travel further into the continent, you'll find that the landscape is also different from what you thought. It's full of mirages, false trails. You'll find that this landscape is already peopled by an indigenous population which you will need to take account of. They have their own demands and their own way of being, which perhaps fits this place better than the characters you are trying to import.

When, after months of struggle, the novel has been created, when the dust of all the arguments between your conscious and your subconscious has settled and there is a definite land mapped out and on the page, that land will seem altogether more vast and more complex than you thought possible. And the fact that it is not the place you thought it was will nag at you. You'll want to tinker and fix things, and in fixing things you will find that you've upset the whole ecosystem of this new world. Then, when trying to fix these imbalances, you will find others that need fixing, too, and so on, until eventually you must leave it alone because there are other worlds to explore, other novels that need your attention.

It's at this point that readers begin to tramp through and they will see a different place from you. They will bring their own histories, their own prejudices, and their own characters. Some, like inquisitive backpackers, will want to get away from the roads through the novel you have created for them; they will be more interested in places that you yourself hardly noticed were there. Others will drift without comment past the beautiful parts of this world, the bits that you yourself are most proud of, seemingly in a hurry just to get to the end of the tour.

The rewards

Building a novel is perhaps the greatest challenge a writer can embark upon. You will need all the skills of a diplomat and the drive, tenacity and ruthless efficiency of a megalomaniac. It is also, of course, hugely rewarding and hugely exciting. As you embark on the journey of the novel, you are Shackleton, Captain Scott, Edmund Hillary, David Livingstone, Columbus, Neil Armstrong, Captain Cook, Ellen MacArthur and Nelson Mandela. You are a statesman–explorer and you don't even have to leave your living room.

First steps

A straight literary novel is between 70,000 and 200,000 words, with most coming in at about 100,000. Before starting down this long road you need to decide what kind of book you are going to write. This does not mean simply what genre you are going to write in – crime, historical, romantic, science or literary fiction – but what your book is going to be about. You also need to decide why it needs to be written.

Why write a novel?

In not more than 100 words, write down exactly why you want to write a novel and who you hope will read it. This will help clarify in your mind your aims and objectives.

Focus point

There are about a million manuscripts in the offices of London or New York literary agents at any one time. Only a fraction of these get published. Don't let that put you off, however. None of those novels is your novel. None of them is written with your voice. None of them says what only you can say. But it is best to be clear about what exactly it is you want to say and why the novel is the best way to say it.

The theme

What is your story going to be about? Your theme is a single word or a short phrase that encapsulates the essence of the story. Being clear about this right at the outset, before you've thought about plot, setting or characters, will help you stay focused and prevent your novel becoming a sprawling mess. It will prevent you being led off at tangents and into culs-de-sac. It may, with any luck, save you time later when it comes to editing (it probably won't but you can always hope).

Dianne Doubtfire

'A book without a theme can become a mere sequence of events with no foundation, no reason for existence.'

Whatever your theme is, keep it in your mind's eye as a light to guide you through the path of your story. Your theme will probably be something you have personal experience of. A passionate desire to communicate experience and knowledge will give your book an inner heat, a propulsive motor that will keep it going.

A novel is not an autobiography and having your theme shining ahead of you as you write will help you cut out those parts of your life story that don't fit. It will also help to remind you to make sure that you alter details of your life as you need to. Like a good tabloid editor, you mustn't let the facts get in the way of a good story. As we have seen, 'Write what you know' is good advice for a writer but its opposite – 'Write what you don't know' – can be important, too. Making stuff up is part of a fiction writer's job and one you shouldn't shy away from. One important difference between fictive lives and our own lives is that in fiction everything has to mean something. This is often not the case in real life.

Write down your themes

Write down five themes that you feel qualified to tackle. Now circle two of these as contenders for the theme of your first book.

Viewpoints

Conventional wisdom has it that the easiest kind of book to write is one with an omniscient third-person narrator. This is a God figure able to see into the minds of all the characters and to follow them all. However, a limited narrator with access to only parts of the story is simpler to write and can often be more effective. As a new novelist, you should try to keep things simple, and match ambition to your limited experience. Admittedly, this will give you some problems later on because you can only tell the reader things that your narrator would know. You can only get to know the characters through him or her. But this very straitjacket means that you are forced to keep things tightly focused.

MULTIPLE NARRATORS

If you have more than one narrator, what you will find is that readers prefer some voices to others. Your readers' attention will flag a little when a narrator takes over whom they don't warm to. This happens even in great books like Jonathan Franzen's *The Corrections* or Irvine Welsh's *Trainspotting*, both of which are first-person novels told by more than one character. In Franzen's book the story takes place over many years and is told by various members of a dysfunctional family, while Welsh's novel is narrated by the various denizens of an Edinburgh housing estate. Even in these great novels with great voices, still some narrators appeal more than others.

WHOSE STORY IS IT?

There is a saying that 'character is story'. It is the characters that will drive your plot. But not all characters will have equal weight. Your novel is not a democracy. Even if you decide to write in the third person you will still need to have a central character in whom the readers can invest their emotional energy. Even if this central character is unlikeable, evil even, we want to see the world through their eyes.

The main character

Just as it is easier with a first book to stick to the first person and a theme that you have experience of, it is probably also a help to have a likeable – if flawed – central character. Too nice and we won't find them plausible or interesting, but if they are too unlikeable then we will become irritated. We won't want to spend much time in their company.

Write your hero

Keeping your theme in mind, write brief character sketches for six of your principal characters (any more than six major characters and you risk losing control of them entirely). Now who, out of this collection, deserves to be the central character? Who is going to be the hero of this book? Choose carefully because this person is going to stay with you night and day for months or years. They are going to have to be fascinating to you now, and grow more fascinating as the story develops. Having the wrong central character is probably what prevents first novels getting off the ground more than almost any other fault (except, possibly, over-ambition).

The voice

Finding the voice of your central character is key to unlocking the story. A strong, engaging voice propels the storyline and hooks the reader in. Some examples of strong voices are:

- Rob, the melancholy music obsessive in Nick Hornby's *High Fidelity*
- Judith Bastiaanz, the naive young Dutch émigrée to the New World whose disastrous first infatuation helps destroy her family in Kathryn Heyman's *The Accomplice*

- the dizzy but determined Bridget in Helen Fielding's *Bridget Jones's Diary*
- Holden Caulfield in J. D. Salinger's *The Catcher in the Rye*, the prototype of every moody teenage narrator we have had since the 1950s (Caulfield's direct descendant is the unlucky Vernon in D. B. C. Pierre's Booker Prize-winning *Vernon God Little*)
- Bessy Buckley, the wide-eyed, sassy nineteenth-century hero in Jane Harris's *The Observations* has a rollicking voice that carries the whole novel
- Christopher, the maths prodigy with Asperger's Syndrome in Mark Haddon's groundbreaking *The Curious Incident of the Dog in the Night-time*
- the earnest and wise Scout in *To Kill a Mockingbird*.

In all these stories a strong narrative voice has been established right at the beginning of the book and sustained through to the end. All the characters mentioned above have flaws (except just possibly the child, Scout) but none of them are unlikeable. Holden Caulfield can seem alienated and difficult but that is exactly why he has exercised such a pull on the psyche of generations of teenagers.

All these narrators have a voice that is vivid, alive and unique. They share the fact that they look at the world in unusual, albeit very different ways.

Voice is probably the hardest of skills to master. It is certainly the hardest to explain, which is why so many different examples are listed above. It's important to get it right. A wrong note in the voice of your narrator and you will quickly begin to lose the trust of your readership.

Peter Plate

'Look for repetitions, rhythm, cadence, pacing (setting something up, bringing it to a close). Look for texture in sentences.'

Even if you decide to write your book in the third person, you will still need to have a voice. An invisible narrator is actually impossible: readers will be responding to a narrative voice, whether or not it is that of an actual character. Voice in this context may be a synonym for style. Look at the novels of Fay Weldon or E. L. Doctorow to see how the third-person novel still requires the push of a powerful narrative voice.

Experiment with voice

Experiment with the voices of your central characters. Have each of them recount an incident from their childhood in their own words. This will be a good way to test whether or not your central character is the right one. Try to make their voices as distinct from each other as you can.

Focus point

Accents and dialect should be implied by the choice of vocabulary. Unless you're Irvine Welsh, writing out accents phonetically doesn't really work. Even if you are Irvine Welsh, it doesn't always work – his London characters are never as convincing in terms of their accent as his Scottish ones.

Structure

Aspiring writers worry about structure more than they worry about anything else. It's as though the word 'structure' holds the same sense of arcane unknowable magic as the words 'quantum physics'. And yet the mechanics of story structure are relatively straightforward. Most books, plays, films and television dramas are written with a three-act structure. And this phrase in itself seems to be a posh way of saying: 'beginning, middle and end'.

THREE ACTS, THREE KINDS OF PLOT

The plot is the journey of your characters through these three acts. There are, essentially, three kinds of plot. The first is the most familiar.

- **The linear plot**
  A linear plot is where the action moves straightforwardly through the acts, the tension building until a climax in the final act. This kind of plotting is familiar to us from many an action movie, as well as many classic novels.

The other two kinds of plot are cyclic. In other words, the position at the end of the book resembles that at the start, except that all the characters are utterly changed.

- **The heroic cycle**
  Familiar to us from the great epics such as *The Odyssey*, this follows the pattern of: Departure, Initiation and Return (think of the structure of *The Hobbit*).

- **The mythic journey**
  This can be expressed as: Cage, Escape, Quest, Dragon and Home (think of the structure of *Watership Down* – warned by a vision of impending catastrophe, a group of young rabbits decide to leave their threatened warren (Cage); they get away despite the best and brutal efforts of the authorities to stop them (Escape); they then search for exactly the right place to set up a new warren (Quest), defeating the fearsome Nazi warren run by General Woundwort (Dragon); finally they end their days in bounty, together with the does they liberated from the enemy warren (Home).

Another way of thinking about this kind of structure might be as three acts containing five parts, these parts being: Inciting incident, Complication, Betrayal, Climax and Resolution. Act One would contain the Inciting incident and the Complication, things heat up with a Betrayal in Act Two, and Act Three would contain the Climax but also the Resolution.

Sketch your plot

Take your central character on a journey using one or more of the plot types described above. What type is going to best suit your theme? Just sketch it out for now.

Setting

This is where your novel takes place and when. We'll look at this in more detail in the next chapter, but it is worth thinking a little about this right at the planning stage of your novel.

You have a theme and a collection of characters and a rough idea of the type of journey that they might undertake. You might want to jot down now the kind of locations where scenes might take place.

Setting is crucial

Novels are best written in scenes. We don't need to know everything that happens in your character's life. We want the important moments, and the setting for these important moments is going to be crucial.

GET YOUR FACTS STRAIGHT

You will want to choose the kinds of settings that you yourself know well. If you know Edinburgh and you know council offices, then utilize this knowledge. Likewise, if you know college radio stations and you know Berkeley, then utilize that knowledge too. The reader will want to trust that you know what you're talking about. The same is true of historical periods: if you are writing a novel about the past, then you owe it to your readers to have researched thoroughly the time in which your book is set. This is true even if you lived through the era about which you are writing. The memory is an unreliable muscle and you will need to go and check your facts. Make sure that you have the right prime minister in power, or that people really were sending emails in 1993.

TIME PERIODS

Another big decision to make is over what time period your story is going to unfold. Is it over decades, as with the classic great American novels like *The World According To Garp*? Or is it just one day, like James Joyce's *Ulysses* or Ian McEwan's *Saturday*?

Whatever you decide, thinking about how the weather changes and how the seasons affect the lives of your characters will help give you a sense of how your story might unfold. Farmers are perhaps the most affected by these kinds of changes, but shopkeepers must plan for Christmas and Halloween. Schoolteachers plan for examination periods. Everyone is affected by the nights drawing in and the weather getting colder and wetter. In India, or America, or Africa, the seasons are different and will affect your characters in different ways. The rhythm of the world they inhabit must affect your characters in some way.

Teach something

For many, part of the pleasure of reading novels is learning something new. In a great novel one will learn about the world, about human nature, about oneself and about different time periods. But there are other, more low-key pleasures to be had. The novels of John Murray teach about life in contemporary Cumbria; *The Electric Michelangelo* by Sarah Hall is fascinating on the evolution of tattooing; the novels of George MacDonald Fraser are the best kind of historical writing, with painstakingly researched facts set in the context of exhilarating action; *Trainspotting* is fascinating on the world of Scottish junkies; while Nicholas Royle's *Antwerp* brings to vivid life the demi-monde of a city about which no one outside Belgium knows very much.

If you have special knowledge about something, whether it is breeding pedigree cats or manufacturing illicit drugs, giving the readers access to this kind of information is actually a kind of generosity.

Story, story, story

It often comes as something of a shock to those attending writing courses that 80,000 beautiful words do not make a novel.

It is true that your characters generate the story but you are not writing lengthy character studies. There must be constant movement, ceaseless surprising progressions. Just as much modern music now seeks to wring the maximum out of each chord before moving a tune forward, thus sacrificing melody and urgency, so many emerging novelists forget that what keeps us turning the pages is a story.

Novelists, even the most serious ones, are in the entertainment business. We are purveyors of pleasure as well as knowledge. It is a complicated, complex kind of pleasure but pleasure nevertheless. Ford Madox Ford wrote that each line of the novel should push it forward. Things have to happen, your characters need to make things happen and then respond to things that other characters do and say. They can't stand still and they shouldn't reflect for too long or too often, unless reflecting for too long is part of their essence, in which case it should have troubling consequences for them. A novel is a sophisticated form of fairground. In the hands of a good novelist you should get the visceral thrills of the rollercoaster, combined with the darker arts of the illusionist. Things have to happen.

Focus point

Go back to the books you love for their quieter, more reflective qualities and note down what actually happens in each book. You'll be surprised how many deaths, infidelities and hurts of all kinds there are. This is true even in Anne Tyler, even in Jane Austen come to that.

Don't get it right, get it written

I don't know who said this first, but it is excellent advice for those starting out on the journey of writing a novel. Too many new writers begin their first chapter in the white heat of creativity and then polish and hone and tweak that opening over and over until it's shining. In the meantime, months have passed and the momentum of the story has been lost.

Bash it down; get it on the page. Forget the critic on your shoulder who has tried to stop you doing anything worthwhile since you were born, and is not helpful at this stage in your life. You will go back and edit and change and tweak and redraft and suffer all the agonies associated with that stage, but for now you need to draw up a realistic schedule for blasting out that first draft. Let it burst out without worrying about coherence or structure or spelling or paragraphing. Get it done. Get it out of you. The real work of the novelist begins with the redrafting. Nevertheless, a bit of planning will help you put your first draft down with minimal risk of becoming blocked.

MAKE A PLAN

You're serious about writing a novel, so draw up a plan of campaign. Set yourself a deadline. Think about how long you've got to write this novel. (Don't think 'the rest of my life': people on the courses I run often say they have spent nearly ten years writing their book. That kind of confession makes my blood run cold.) You'll need time to plot, time to develop your characters, time to work on the setting, time to write a synopsis and then you'll need to write a first draft. And of course you'll need time to do all the other things in your life – work, family, exercise. Writing your novel shouldn't cost you any of these; that's too high a price to pay.

By now you should have an established writing routine. Break the task of getting this novel down into chunks and stick to the schedule you've set yourself, whether that is six weeks of planning followed by a chapter a week or another schedule which is manageable for you. Write it on the calendar and pin it somewhere prominent.

Focus point

Tell as many people as possible that you are writing a novel. This makes all those who might sabotage your plan part of your team. If people feel involved in your struggle, they might not be so insistent about breaking into your writing time.

If all has gone to plan and you have been following the advice given so far, you should now be ready to begin writing your first chapter.

Write the first chapter

Write the first chapter of your novel. Don't give everything away at once. Remember what Charles Reade wrote in his nineteenth-century writing manual *Advice to Young Authors on Writing Novels*: 'Make 'em laugh; make 'em cry; make 'em wait.'

Workshop exercise

When you've written your first chapter, send it to the drawer for at least a couple of weeks. Then read through it again, carefully, several times. As you're reading, try to answer the following questions, which should help you make sure you've covered all the points in this chapter.

1. Are you happy with the viewpoint from which your story is told? If you've chosen first person, try rewriting a passage in third, and vice versa. Is this an improvement or not? You don't have to stick with your first choice of viewpoint. You're in charge here.

2. Read your chapter out loud. I always say this, but it really is the best way to identify any clumsy sentences or dodgy dialogue. Is there anything that just doesn't sound right to you? Highlight it to work on later.

3. Do you like your main character? Do they sound on the page the same as you hear them in your head? Is there a better perspective from which to tell your story? As you are writing you may find that other characters pipe up and demand you listen to their stories, too. Hear them out; they may have something interesting to say.

4. Do you begin with a bang, with action, with something that will hook your reader in from the first page? If your first chapter builds up to a big event, consider reworking it so that your readers find themselves in the heat of the moment from the start.

5. Does your first chapter evoke a sense of place? Would a first-time reader know where they are? Remember to engage all the senses; don't just describe what your character can see.

Edit your chapter

Now take the notes you made in the workshop and apply them to your first chapter. You may want to rewrite it completely. You may just want to amend the odd paragraph. When you think you've finished, go back to the beginning of the workshop and do it all again.

Where to next?

Now that we've looked at the basics of novel writing, from deciding on a theme to producing a tentative first chapter, it's time to move on and have a look in a little more detail at setting, characterization and plotting.

10

Taking your novel
further

In the previous chapter we looked at how a novel is conceived, from the first whisper of an idea to a tentative first chapter. Now we're going to explore some of the most important aspects of novel writing in a little more detail.

In this chapter you will learn more about the role that setting should play in your story and how to create a visual style. There is advice on how to create believable characters and dialogue that sparkles and moves the plot forward. You'll also learn more about the 12 classic plots and about planning your work as a series of scenes, to give yourself a scene breakdown similar to those used by screenwriters.

Even if you've decided that writing a novel is not for you, you'll still find plenty of advice you can use in other forms of writing.

The importance of place

The places in which your stories take place can be vital to their success. In many of the best novels the setting is almost a character in the book. The India of Forster's *A Passage to India*, the Edinburgh of Ian Rankin's detective novels, the Yorkshire moorland of *Wuthering Heights*, the small towns and suburbs of the USA brought to life by John Updike, the island in William Golding's *Lord of the Flies*: all of these are stories where the texture of the setting illuminates the action and the characters.

It isn't simply landscapes that can provide evocative locations: think of the hospital ward in Ken Kesey's *One Flew over the Cuckoo's Nest* or the oppressive school in Zoë Heller's *Notes on a Scandal*. Both of these institutional settings help to brew a feeling of claustrophobia in which the characters are trapped. The settings are so authentically drawn that we feel we can trust the writer to pilot us skilfully through the plot, too.

Don't worry if you think your chosen settings are too bleak or too unromantic. The grim English steel town of Corby was the setting for John Burnside's aptly titled *Living Nowhere*, a novel that works precisely because of the sense of small-town, dead-end ennui that rises from the pages.

Jean de la Bruyère

'Making books is a craft, like making clocks: it takes more than wit to be an author.'

IMAGINARY LOCATIONS

As we've said before, it helps if your setting is a place you know well, but some places you are inventing from scratch and with these it is, paradoxically, all the more important that you get them right. If you get a street name wrong in a real town, people will no doubt write you a pained letter, but if your world is entirely fictitious then it must feel truthful.

In creating a new world, you don't have the luxury of looking places up on an A–Z street map. You must overcome the reader's natural scepticism about things that are obviously made up by giving them a fully realized place. It must feel that you at least have been there, even if no one else has. And of course, like the set in a film, it mustn't be so distracting as to take our minds away from the story.

Interweaving a sense of place so that it adds to the momentum of a novel is one of the most difficult tricks for a novelist to pull off.

Describing imaginary places can be one of the most satisfying aspects of the fiction writer's job – so much so that it is often one of the areas where we are apt to get carried away and ladle on far too much. The readers start to buckle under the strain of it and their heads start to throb with sensory overload. With descriptions of setting, like so much else in both life and writing, less is more. Limit yourself. Try to make a habit of interspersing description with action.

Creating believable characters

The easiest mistake you can make when developing characters is to think that you can just put yourself and the people you know into a book. This is reckless because it can get you sued, but it is also a way of crippling yourself right from the start. Fiction is about making stuff up, including the people. A piece of fiction that is thinly disguised autobiography often fails on both counts. It fails to grip in the way that a fully realized story can, and fails to convince as autobiography should. Begun dishonestly, the story will hit false notes all the way through and will prove an unsatisfactory read.

Luigi Pirandello

'When the characters are really alive before their author, the latter does nothing but follow them in their action, in their words, in the situation which they suggest to him.'

YOURSELF AS YOUR MODEL?

It is particularly unwise to use yourself as the sole model for your central character. This is because it is unlikely that you really know yourself well enough to produce a version that convinces in a book. Everyone's idea of themselves is wrong in so many ways. In fact, the proper job of a human being could be said to be getting to know yourself, and that is a lifetime's work. Writing novels might be part of that process, but making yourself the leading character in them probably isn't.

LOVE YOUR MAIN CHARACTER

It is essential that you feel affection for your central character, even if no one else does. Jane Austen wrote of the clever but vain Emma Woodhouse, the eponymous heroine of *Emma*, 'I have written a heroine whom no one but myself will much like.' (The author is not quite fair to poor Emma. She might be wilful, irritating, and not as bright as she thinks she is, but she is kind-hearted and cheerful and, in the end, able to laugh at herself while learning from her mistakes.) So don't use your book to take vengeance on those who have crossed you. At least don't grant them the importance of making them central characters. Relegate your enemies to relatively unimportant parts of the story. That will be far more wounding to them. One of the curious by-products of fiction writing is that people often want to see themselves in books, even if the characters they think most resemble them are distinctly unlikeable.

Your characters should have faults and weaknesses, but it is up to the readers to work these out. You are merely their guide. Readers want to be doing the principal legwork themselves. Like determined hikers, readers want to get to the summit under their own steam. They don't want to be carried. Your task as writer is to discreetly stop your readership drifting away from the paths you want them to take. And, like a tour guide, you can't shape your readers' reactions to the sights they see as they progress through your story. They may pick up things you haven't noticed and have very different feelings from you about the view from the top.

You have two stories

All stories are written twice: once by the writer and once by the reader. And your readers will have a different relationship from you to the characters you create. They may like some more, and others less.

Here is another of Martyn Bedford's exercises designed to help you create a believable character and to get right away from allowing your own personality to hog the limelight in your own story. You'll have a lot of fun with this.

Create a character

1   Note down a list of between five and ten words that you think might most accurately describe your main personality traits.

2   Beside these words write their opposites.

3   Using this second list, imagine yourself to be that person.

4   In that role, imagine that you are now applying for a place in the Big Brother house and write a video-diary monologue about yourself, saying why you should be allowed in.

CHOOSING NAMES

It's hard for a character to live in your mind until you have found their name. Anyone who has named children (or even pets!) knows how important it is to get this right. Choosing a name is not a rational project but one that employs instinct and gut feeling. And when it comes to choosing fictional characters you have some additional problems. The names that you choose for villains shouldn't be libellous; that is, the readers mustn't confuse Valerie Jones, the serial bigamist of your novel, with the real-life Valerie Jones who teaches piano in Bedford.

Many writers frequent graveyards in search of both names and unpleasant causes of death. Graveyards are also good for reminding yourself to crack on with the book. There may not be as much time to get it finished as you thought!

Good sources of names are www.babycentre.com, which provides lists of the top ten baby names for each state of the United States, and www.babynames.co.uk, which gives information on names in the UK. And then there is always the telephone directory.

DESCRIBING YOUR CHARACTERS

It was once the convention to spend a long time describing characters. If you are a devotee of Victorian novels, you will know how pages can be taken up describing a character and their background. Nowadays we try to show character through action rather than tell the reader about it. A few phrases should be enough. Remember that the readers want to use their own imaginations while reading your book; that is, after all, the great pleasure of reading as opposed to watching television or films.

It is often the most unusual details that are the most evocative. Everyone has their idiosyncrasies and you should be on the lookout for these, ready to incorporate them into your characters. These quirks of personality or movement are more likely to show up if you have your characters actively involved in the story rather than simply giving a general description.

POSSESSIONS

What people have, or what they aspire to, often says a great deal about them. We make snap judgements about people based on what they wear, but also on what else they own. Who hasn't browsed the bookshelves or music collection of a new acquaintance looking for clues to their character to emerge through their tastes? And a person who dreams of owning a vintage 2CV complete with a 'Nuclear Power No Thanks' sticker is likely to be a different kind of person from a Rolex-wearing BMW driver. Everything that people possess is the result of a distinct choice: muesli or Coco Pops in the cupboard; full-fat or skimmed milk; black coffee or weak tea for breakfast; supermarket own-brand whisky or Laphroaig; trainers or handmade brogues; Armani or Oxfam; the Sex Pistols or Mahler; *Mad Men* or *Curb Your Enthusiasm*; and all the various possible choices in between.

Characters can make inaccurate guesses about others, based on the flimsy evidence of their possessions. Thinking about what your characters own can be a great way to make them become real, while their possessions may also give you a way of surprising your readers. Surprise is important because readers will be second-guessing you every step of the way, trying to work out the twists and turns of your plot. Your characters must remain believable, but they must also be capable of changing and of doing the unexpected, at least occasionally.

Your character's things

1 Write a list of 25 things that one of your characters might own. Don't spend too long thinking about it. Let your unconscious do at least some of the work here.

2 Now choose five of those items and write down how your character came by them.

3 Now choose one object that your character might prize above all the others and write a short scene describing what happens when that object goes missing.

MOTIVE AND DESIRE

One of the things that will give your story momentum is deciding what your characters want from life. It might be more or better possessions, as outlined above. It is more likely to be the things that objects represent – that is, power and status. Or it might be fame or love or security for the family. Some things your characters may not even be able to articulate. They may be subconscious, primeval urges: sweet old ladies can be driven by a sibling rivalry that started in infancy; a daughter may want her father's approval; a politician may be trying to make up for the fact that he had no power at school. Subconscious drives are the essence of good dramas. It is worth thinking about what your characters most desire right at the beginning of any kind of story.

Whether they are striving to achieve their desires themselves, trying to protect their current position or responding to the actions of others, it is this response to deep drives and yearnings that will provide much of the impulse of your story. It is the constant struggle to resolve the deepest urges that will result in change in your characters. We've learned already that there can be no such thing as still life.

Struggle and change

Change and growth are inevitable and necessary in fictional characters, just as they are in reality.

Workshop exercise

In this exercise we'll work on developing your characters by examining their desires.

- What do your main characters want out of life? Take each one in turn and write this down in simple sentences.
- What is preventing them from achieving this?
- What will happen if they can't get to where they want to be? What will they do if they can't fulfil their dreams?
- Achieving your desires can of course be just the start of some serious trouble. Macbeth becomes king of Scotland but his life spirals downwards from there. And the modern tabloid world is littered with celebrity casualties unable to cope with getting what they wished for. Imagine that your central characters have achieved their desires. What is the worst thing that could happen to them as a result?
- Write a short story that shows the unravelling of a life that should have been perfect.

In the end, thinking about your characters 'off the page', outside the story itself, may help you move along faster when you do come to write your novel.

Mavis Cheek

'Characters are organic to your plot and all the best fiction is character led. When you have your story, you should know, in outline, who's going to be in it and what their function is. Details come later. For filling the character out there is no better place to observe human life than on a Tube train or in a café. Just sit there and see who comes in and imagine what their inner life is – and how their outer appearance feeds those ideas of yours. But all mine come from out of my head. With bits and pieces of people I really know attached here and there.'

(Mavis Cheek is the author of many very successful novels including Patrick Parker's Progress and The Sex Life of My Aunt (Faber and Faber).)

Plotting

Chapter 9 includes a little about plotting and gave you three basic storylines that are useful when you are first beginning. Now it's time to add to your armoury. A lot of people seem to agree that there are actually seven basic plots and that all stories are variations of these. This is a thesis developed by Christopher Booker in his influential work *The Seven Basic Plots: Why We Tell Stories* (Continuum Books, 2004). However, other writers identify a few more.

Here are 12 templates for plots that writers return to again and again:

1 **Killing the Dragon** – whereby your hero or community faces a terrible threat and after a great struggle saves their family, community, or indeed the whole world from annihilation.

2 **Rags to Riches** – where the underdogs draw on inner qualities and triumph against all the odds.

3   The Quest or Journey – this is the heroic form we came across earlier, where our heroes leave their home to find treasure. This doesn't have to be money; it could be a missing child or a sacred object (remember King Arthur and the Holy Grail).

4   Voyage and Return – this is similar to the other heroic cycles mentioned earlier, where the protagonist leaves the life they know, their home, family and friends, in order to go to strange lands, and returns via strange adventures.

5   Comedy – where confusion, misunderstandings and mutual incomprehension stop a character achieving their desires. This should turn out happily in the end.

6   Tragedy – whereby a character has some fatal flaw that undermines them as they struggle to achieve their goals. Despite all their qualities, there is something within which stops the hero achieving. Or perhaps the goal was out of reach in the first place. Ultimately the hero overreaches. Think of Thomas Hardy's *Jude the Obscure* or *Macbeth*.

7   Rebirth – a character undergoes a complete transformation in order to get what they want.

8   Rite of Passage – the problems, traumas and painfully necessary learning experiences associated with growing up.

9   Rebellion – a character, community or group launches a struggle against authority.

10   The Switch – two characters swap lives.

11   The Faustian Pact – a character makes a bargain that they cannot get out of.

12   Rise and Fall – a character loses everything and must begin again from scratch. Often, despite everything, the protagonist succeeds in getting back to the top.

It is natural to worry about originality, but these plots are as old as writing itself, and have been developed in a countless variety of ways. Whatever plot you use, it is your characters, your personal history, your style and thoughts that will make it unique.

Use a basic plot idea

You have probably got quite a lot of ideas for stories in your notebook. Some of them will just be odd lines of overheard dialogue, or notes about a character you want to put into a story. Others will be a few words based around a theme. Still others will be more fully fleshed out than this. Try to pick out an idea and fit it to one of the basic plot ideas outlined above. Try it on several of them, all of them even. You should find that each plot will turn your scrap of an idea into a quite new, but considerably more developed, story.

Planning

Once you've got your central characters, your theme and your basic plot, it is tempting just to start writing. For most people this is probably a mistake. It will be a lot easier if you think of your book as a series of scenes. Try to give yourself a scene breakdown in a similar way to those used by screenwriters. Then plan the beginning, middle and end of each scene. Aim to produce a one-page outline for each scene before you begin writing it. Try to think about what each character wants to get from the scene (not all characters will feature in every scene, of course).

Keep a visual chart of the progress each of your main characters makes through the story. A lot of writers do this on a large piece of paper, or by having index cards that they can stick to a wall. What you are essentially doing here is mapping your story. It is something that you can return to in order to avoid getting lost or sidetracked.

Creating a visual map will mean that you can make sure your characters are leading a properly chequered existence. If one character seems to be sailing pretty plainly through your book, then you will need to create setbacks and disasters. Some characters must be rising as others are falling, and if these vicissitudes can be tracked at a glance, you will find that you stay focused.

Having a clear and colourful plan (buy lots of marker pens or felt tips!) will also help you as your characters move towards a climax. If you put this climax down on your map, then it gives you an end point. Tension should build in your story. There is a sense in which all books should be thrillers.

SUSPENSE

Suspense is the art of not answering readers' questions. You are delaying gratification in order that they have a more satisfactory pay-off later on. You are also giving readers the pleasure of writing the book along with you. You are making them work, and readers – masochists that they are – enjoy that. Writing a book is always a collaborative act between you and your readers. You have to give them room to contribute.

Many new writers give away everything about the plot and the characters in the opening chapter. You can give a lot less information than you might expect. On the other hand, objects and people mentioned early should return later. Nothing should be wasted. You are going to need to resolve all the journeys on which the characters embark. This is another argument in favour of your colourful wallchart. You should be able to see at a glance where your characters have got to.

WRITER AS SADIST

You are going to have to be mean to your characters, even the ones you like. In fact, be especially mean to the ones you like. Your characters must labour under the burdens of problems to start with, and these should get worse before they get better. And even when they get better this should often prove to be a false dawn. You have to treat your characters mean in order to keep your readers keen.

You'll need to keep a ready eye out for stories of the kind that can fall – like rain – into a person's life.

 Treat 'em mean

Sad but true: an interest in human disasters and frailty is essential in a novelist.

Murdering your babies

Writing is a brutal job. It's exhausting, frustrating and upsetting. And one of the most upsetting things about it can be the need to kill off your characters. Sometimes, in order to move things along, you are going to have to make dramatic, surprising and risky decisions. Somewhere along the line there will come a point when you have to sacrifice a favourite son. And by sacrifice, we really do mean 'kill'. Novels are worlds where the same stuff happens as happens in any world: births, marriages, love, sex, work and friendship, but also divorce, disease, accidents, death and crime.

Focus point

Readers want chills as well as thrills and part of your job is to give those to them.

But there is another, perhaps better, reason for killing off some of your favourite characters. It can free you up. Just as some widows and widowers blossom after the death of a partner, however beloved that partner was – developing new skills and interests that surprise those who knew them before – so you as a novelist might be liberated by having to allow some of the other characters to work harder.

We're not advocating killing off your hero early on. That seems foolhardy. Getting rid of a hero in whom your readers have invested significant emotional capital seems a reckless and difficult trick to pull off. But there may be a secondary character who can threaten to unbalance a book, who takes up just too much room. Getting rid of them might provide a surprising twist but also allow a period of calm and reflection, after which those characters that are left can assume control of the story.

Focus point

Being forced from your comfort zone into the company of characters you feel less at ease with may well benefit your book as a whole.

SUBPLOTS

A subplot is a story that echoes or contrasts with the central narrative of your book. It may well involve minor characters in more central positions. Imagine that you have a story where a domineering husband leaves the family home to go and fight in a war. Your major plot might concern itself with his wife becoming independent as she starts to do the things that he did before. Perhaps she gets a job, or starts meeting other men, or discovers other possibilities in her life. She starts to grow, develop and change. It is a difficult time for the country but a liberating time for her. A subplot might concern itself with the relationships her children build up while their mother is working and their father is away. Perhaps they develop an unexpected rapport with the father's mother, which will cause conflict later in the book when the father returns from fighting and expects everything to be the same as it was when he left.

Your subplot needs to be satisfying in itself, but you don't want it to overwhelm the action. Remember that the theme of your subplot will work best if it is a different – perhaps very different – take on the theme of your book as a whole.

Subplots provide satisfying diversions away from the main action while at the same time giving the reader another oblique perspective on it. They also heighten the suspense by taking the narrative in a new direction just as the reader felt they were going to get some resolution.

TO PLAN OR NOT TO PLAN

We have spent a long time considering different methods of planning a novel. Some writers hardly plan at all. John Fowles said, 'I begin with an image, a ghost of an idea, nothing more, not knowing where it will lead.' Iris Murdoch, on the other hand, planned everything in great detail. Most novelists fall somewhere between these two positions. As a novelist I tend to have a loose plan based around my ghost of an idea, but I fully expect it to change as I progress and as the characters begin to seize control. I then wrest control back in the redrafts before eventually letting my characters do what they are compelled to do in the end. However, I am still learning as a writer and I hope my techniques will become varied as I progress. Perhaps my next book will be one where I plan absolutely every detail. And maybe the one after that will be the one where I start with just a title and nothing else.

Rewrite or plan

Whatever kind of writer you are, the less planning you do
before your first draft, the more extensive your rewrites will be.

Beginnings are easy;
endings are hard

Anyone can start a novel, but keeping going and completing it is the
preserve of the dedicated. You have to decide what kind of ending you
want. Just as in a short story, you have the option of a closed ending
where everything is tied up, or an open ending where the possibilities
for the characters stretch out into a future that is unwritten, except
in the mind of the reader who has just finished the story. You want
to avoid the reader thinking, 'So what?' They have invested a good
chunk of time and emotional energy into the book and they want to
feel richly compensated for this. They want a return.

So how do you know when, finally, to give readers what they crave?
Essentially, your characters will tell you. When they have solved
their major problems and moved on, ready to start a new phase in
life, that's when you should stop too.

Here is another exercise from the great Martyn Bedford that allows
you to test just how far you have come in beginning to think
seriously about your novel.

Write a scene

Select an incident from your childhood and write it as a brief
scene (you may be faithful to the actual incident or you may
fictionalize). You are free to write it from the child's perspective, or
from that of another participant or witness, and to choose either
of the narrative viewpoints (i.e. first or third person). Pay attention
to feelings and emotion as well as to dialogue, description and
action – the purpose is to combine place/setting, characterization
and event/situation in one short piece of prose.

Dialogue

Alice (in Wonderland) wondered, 'What is the use of a book without pictures or conversation?' And she's got a point. The conversation in your fiction is hugely important in helping give your story pace and sparkle. Dialogue in fiction is used to convey information, to move the plot and to provide us with a richer understanding of the characters. But what you can't do in fiction is simply write speech as it occurs in real life. Students new to writing often defend tedious dialogue by arguing that they copied it down verbatim from an exchange they heard on a bus or in a café. But if you are going to write speech exactly as it occurs in normal human discourse, you are going to have a very long, very boring book.

LIFE VERSUS ART

People speaking to one another say 'er' and 'um' and then lose track of what they were saying, and digress and interrupt one another and get distracted. They repeat themselves, they hesitate, repeat themselves again and often go on and on and on and on and on and ... you get the picture.

The paradoxical thing about writing believable dialogue is that you have to get rid of the very things that make it real. Real speech would be hugely complicated to reproduce on the page and would give your reader a migraine.

Roddy Doyle

'I see people in terms of dialogue and I believe that people are their talk.'

Dialogue in a book is there to fulfil two functions: it must move the story forward and it must allow us to get to know the characters better. If it is not doing this, then it is not needed. So keep dialogue short and to the point. Pare it down wherever possible. On the other hand, careful use of speech can save you writing lots of unnecessary description.

152

A sentence like, 'Hey Judy, like that top. Very swirly. And pink. Very you' stops you having to spend ages describing Judy's clothes, and also tells you something about both characters (i.e. Judy likes wearing colourful eccentric clothes and whoever is speaking to her is a patronizing old bag, or maybe just doesn't like her very much). Whatever the case, there's quite a lot going on behind one fairly innocuous line of dialogue.

EXPOSITION

Too much information in speech will make the character sound stilted and false. As a general rule, try to keep a character's lines of dialogue to no more than three uninterrupted sentences at a time. This is a rule you can break occasionally (if you have a long-winded character, or when someone finally spills out words they have been storing up for a long time), but a novel is not really the place for monologues or for wordy exchanges of views.

Focus point

Conversations in books should not be like televised political debates where each person gets sufficient airtime to set out a balanced, logical case. (Sadly, too many are.)

Use a transcript

1 Record five minutes of two of your family or friends speaking.

2 Write out a verbatim transcript.

3 Now rewrite the exchange as though it was a passage in a novel, cutting what you feel is unnecessary and keeping what might move a story on or tell us about character.

HE SAID, SHE SAID

New writers are often seduced into thinking that they should come up with alternatives to 'he said' and 'she said'. The results are always clunky and often comically archaic. Think of this little exchange for example:

'What on Earth is going on?' demanded Julian. 'Julie's gone mad,' exclaimed Sophie. 'I must have Walter or I'll die,' protested Julie. 'That man again!' Julian ejaculated. 'Over my dead body.'

Ridiculous, isn't it? It's only amateur writers who feel the need to find constant alternatives to 'he said'/'she said'. Most established writers use this phrase without it intruding at all, whereas the alternatives always muddy the flow of the text, making it far more awkward than it need be. Often you don't need any attributive verb like 'he said' at all, merely the speech itself, followed by the next one.

 Focus point

The best way to discover whether or not your dialogue is working is to read it aloud.

Mastering voices

Each character should have a distinctive way of speaking. The way someone talks, the grammar, the choice of vocabulary: all of this tells us a lot about them. We learn about social class, about education, about the way they see the world and the way they see themselves from these kinds of clues. Everyone has a unique way of using language and you must be careful that your characters don't bleed into each other.

DIALECTS

Don't be tempted to resolve this problem by using dialect. Obviously a Cockney cabbie must sound like a Cockney cabbie, but do this by his turns of phrase rather than by using apostrophes to replace his missing 'h's. This will be easier to do when you are writing about people and communities familiar to you.

'BAD' LANGUAGE

I have had more complaints about my tendency towards what my Yorkshire friends call 'Effing and Jeffing' than for anything else.

This is particularly true of pieces that I have written for the stage. I don't make any apology for this. Swearing is used as punctuation by whole swathes of people now, and not just underclass characters either. In fact, no one swears quite like the upper classes. In terms of imaginative vulgarity, a graduate of Cheltenham Ladies' College can hold her own with any docker or squaddie.

Sometimes it's hardly believable if characters don't use four-letter words. You should use language truthfully. However, unthinking repetition of profanity, when not used for effect, can grow very tiresome very quickly. You should be aware, too, that words when printed are much louder than when spoken. We might hardly notice when some people we know swear, because they do it so often it's like breathing. But if they were to swear in a letter or email to us, then we'd be quite shocked.

As a writer, you want all your words to have a planned effect, and some profanities can be stored like little bombs and dropped in where they'll do appropriate damage.

See John Cooper Clarke's fantastic poem 'Evidently Chickentown' to see how repetition of a particular swearword (when nicely done!) can be used with devastating brilliance.

Be mindful, though, that this might also be an area where you might have to compromise with a publisher or editor.

CONTEXT

It is important that your reader knows where the conversations are taking place. You don't need to labour the point, but some action to help the reader see the scene is always helpful.

If a vicious argument is taking place in the kitchen, then there are a whole host of actions that the characters might do which might help reveal the way their emotions are moving as the row progresses. Rummaging in the fridge or determinedly making tea as a wife confesses to an affair might show a man trying to hold on to normality or maintain dignity as his world falls apart. Cleaning the floor or getting the kids' tea ready while a husband rambles on about his day at the office can be done in such a way as to show boredom, exasperation, repressed dislike, as can that same wife's non-committal monosyllabic interjections to her husband's talk.

The point is that conversations happen in a setting that the reader wants to be able to picture.

LAYOUT

For layout on the page, study good modern writing and note that a new paragraph is required each time a different character speaks. Action by a character who has just spoken or who is about to speak appears on the same line.

In the UK, single inverted commas are usually employed for dialogue, with double ones for quotes within a speech (e.g. 'I read "Lady with Lapdog" last week.'), but publishers have their own preference and sometimes this procedure is reversed (as in the United States).

Some publishers use dashes. Others use no speech indications at all but make it obvious in the text nevertheless. Look at this example:

> *Get away from me, you ape. Still he comes nearer. I can feel his hot breath close to my cheek. You stink. Go away.*
>
> *That's not very nice, he says. He's trying to smile but it's not really working. I'm not very nice, I say. If I just keep him away from me till Dan arrives. Dan is my boyfriend.*

You see how you can still tell who's talking? If you read enough books, you'll find a contemporary style that you feel happy adopting.

Thoughts should never be put into inverted commas. It's too easy to confuse them with speech. A good technique is to begin the thought with a capital letter: 'She thought, He's no idea what I'm driving at'. You might prefer a colon to a comma after 'She thought'. A good guide to all these punctuation and layout dilemmas is Lynne Truss's *Eats, Shoots & Leaves* (Fourth Estate, 2009).

Rewrite a scene

Write 500 words of dialogue in which two people engage in a violent quarrel. Do it in the form of a play first, with only the two names, the words spoken, and one line to set the scene. Then rewrite with action and setting sketched in, but still keep the length of the overall piece to 500 words.

Where to next?

Now you've seen how to develop your novel further, we're going to move on and look in closer detail at the process of editing your drafts, whether they're drafts of novels, stories, articles or anything else you've been working on.

11

The difficult business of second drafts

All writing is rewriting. No one ever has handed in a first draft, posted it off and sat back to receive the applause and the cheques. In this chapter you will learn how to revise and edit your work in a way that will enable your true voice to shine through. You will discover how to decide what to cut and what to keep and how to go through the revision process in a way that will enhance your unique style. There is information about the enemies of good style and the importance of good grammar and punctuation. For the sake of convenience, this chapter often refers to editing and shaping a novel, but the advice here is universal and will help you revise any piece of writing.

The craft of revision

'First drafts are shit,' said Hemingway, but he should have added that they are necessary shit. I'm a real believer in pouring out a first draft, leaving it to compost for a while and then going over it systematically and ruthlessly. Be your own harshest critic. The chances are that you'll need to revise everything. If you've left enough time between drafts, new and better ideas will have occurred to you already. You'll have accrued new material, much of it deserving of a place in the final text. This is good, because there will also be plenty from the first draft that needs cutting.

Nicolas Boileau

Of every four words I write, I strike out three.

Revising is creative

Cutting, reshaping and reworking may very well be the most creative stage of the whole writing process.

When you embark on the rewriting process, the first thing is to read your work very carefully. Whatever you've written, be it a novel, a memoir or anything else, you'll need to know it inside out. And don't read it on the computer. Make sure you have a hard copy printed double-spaced with a wide margin, so that you can scribble notes and revise phrases. There is something about having real paper in your hand that enables you to spot mistakes much, much more easily than when they are on the screen.

New ideas will occur to you all the time as you read your manuscript and I promise that the craft of revision, which seemed so painful when you began, will quickly begin to create its own exhilarating energy. When you first contemplate revising a piece of work, especially one as large as a book, it can seem like climbing the same hard, high mountain all over again without even the thrill of conquering it to look forward to. You've already seen the view from the summit, you've already had the triumphant glow of having achieved the top. Surely doing it again just gives you the slog without the joy? Fortunately, although there are numerous similarities between writing and mountain climbing, they are not an exact match.

As you progress through your redraft, you will find new routes, new views, new and better ways to express yourself. Your copy of your text will become covered in scribbles and crossings out and hieroglyphs that will mean nothing to you but are your blueprint for the book you were always meant to write.

There will also be times when you smile at your work.

Savour the good moments

It is perfectly acceptable to give yourself a hug, a secret high five. Phrases, scenes, lines of dialogue: every now and again you will stumble over something you've written and be amazed that it came from you. Those are good moments and you should savour them.

When not to murder your babies

In 1914, in *On the Art of Writing*, Sir Arthur Quiller-Couch wrote: 'Whenever you feel an impulse to perpetrate a piece of exceptionally fine writing, obey it – wholeheartedly – and delete it before sending your manuscript to press. Murder your darlings.'

This is crazy, isn't it? Joe Orton said that whenever he came across a piece in his own work that made him laugh out loud, then that is what he would end up cutting. More fool him. Writing is so often difficult and painful that it seems perverse to make it harder than it needs to be. You started writing because there were things only you could say. And because you felt you had a unique way of saying them. Why cut what makes your work special? Why stop doing the thing that you do best? No one thought it was a good idea to put George Best in goal; no one puts the marathon runner Paula Radcliffe in for the 100-metre sprint.

Of course, we have to be alert for work that seems pretentious. And some of your work which seems especially fine on a first or second reading will seem awkward in a third draft when everything around it has changed. But in this context don't kill your babies, nurture them, work on them, improve on them. These stylistic tics may be the very things future readers cherish about your work.

Stick at it

Give yourself a tick every time you come across something in your work that you really really like. Don't cheat; you have to genuinely love it. Then count your ticks. Do the same exercise after a redraft; with any luck the number has gone up significantly. You are doing this as a confidence boost. You are a good writer; stick at it.

Working preferences

We suggested that you write in scenes, and you should revise the same way. Does every scene deserve its place in the piece as a whole and does each sentence within the scene need to be there?

Some writers feel the need to perfect each sentence as far as possible before going on to the next. This is fine. Many of the best writers work this way. I don't. I believe in roughing the work out in full and going back. Others will write out a thousand words in rough in the morning and then edit and revise those words in the afternoon. There are nearly as many working methods as there are writers and there's certainly no right way to go about it. However, you should beware of honing one particular area of your work so much that it holds you up and you never finish. That's the literary equivalent of pruning your hanging baskets while the garden quietly turns into a jungle.

Many new writers have a fantastically polished first chapter and struggle to complete the whole book. Good enough is sometimes good enough.

Beware fear of failure

Perfectionism can simply be fear of failure in a nicer frock. It can be a hindrance. Don't get it right. Get it written.

What all writers should be wary of is just revising on the computer screen. The edit tools are very seductive. The urge to spend all day cutting, pasting and rearranging the text can get in the way of actually doing any writing. It is easy to convince yourself that you are writing when you are in fact simply typing.

Workshop exercise

Choose a piece of writing you have completed. Read through it slowly and ask yourself the following questions:

1. **Have you begun in the right place?** Many novice writers find themselves apologizing to those kind people who have volunteered to be the first readers of a work – 'The story doesn't really get going until chapter three,' they stammer. In which case, chapter three should actually be the first chapter. Amazingly, similar apologies crop up in the covering letters sent with submissions to agents and publishers. There is also that tendency among new writers to give too much away in the first chapter. However, you should aim to grab the reader in the opening passages, whatever genre you are writing in.

2. **Is there too much backstory?** There might well be information about your characters that you need to know but the reader doesn't. We have considered many different ways of creating fully rounded characters, but some of this should inform you as you write, rather than be for the reader to plough through.

3. **Are there any unintentional repetitions?** The answer is almost certainly yes. When you are writing at speed and in the heat of inspiration, this is understandable. So revise with care, eliminating all the words that could undermine the flow of your prose. A more difficult

problem to eradicate might be where you have repeated ideas rather than phrases. It is easy to say the same thing twice, in different ways.

4. **Is anything irrelevant?** Have you included material unrelated to your central theme? Your first draft of your first book may well include a great deal that has personal resonance for you, but which is unnecessary in terms of the plot. It all has to go.

5. **Is your research showing?** This is a particular danger for non-fiction writers, but novelists can suffer from it too. As you get ready to write a book, your reading and trawling through the weirder, wilder reaches of Google will have unearthed all sorts of arcane facts that you'll be tempted to crowbar into your book. Don't. Stories are wiry, tough creatures but they can still be crushed beneath a weight of unnecessary research. Your reader may become frustrated trying to wade through the maze you have created for them. They may give up. The Trivial Pursuits champion at a dinner party, who knows a million facts about every subject that comes up in conversation, may be nice, clever and widely read, yet also unlikely to ever get a girlfriend. In the same way, your book, too, may find itself a wallflower in the library through inflicting too much unnecessary knowledge upon the reader.

6. **Is there any dead wood?** One writer I know sets his students this exercise: they must write for 30 minutes on a set subject and then they must cut every other word. Sometimes the result is gobbledegook, but individual sentences and paragraphs are often improved in surprising ways. Cutting the dead wood is the very essence of good writing. Get rid of whatever is superfluous. Slash and burn. Be ruthless. My hard drive contains 100,000 words of my first book that were never used, the result of four complete drafts. And how do you spot the dead wood? If you have let your manuscript simmer in a drawer, away from prying eyes and sunlight for a good long while, then dead wood will leap out at you. More dead wood will become apparent if you read the work out loud. Also, every sentence over 30 words is almost certainly too long.

If you have spent as much time on revising as you did on writing the book in the first place, you might be tempted to think that now it is finished. It must be. Well, put it away for another few days and come back to it again. There will still be too many words. And when your candid friends have given it the once-over, there will still be more to cut.

There will still be material that embarrasses you whenever you think of it.

Keep what you cut

Some of the words you cut may end up going back in, of course (though probably not that many), and in any case you should keep all the material you throw away. It may contain the bones of further future good work.

Start something new

When you've finished revising the piece you're working on, go back and have a look through the bits you cut. Pick a sentence at random and use it as the starting point for a completely different story.

The art of good style

The point of getting rid of all the clutter is to highlight your style, not to obscure it. If you write in your own way, and do it regularly, you will establish a style you feel comfortable with. Cutting will be part of the process of clearing all that doesn't fit with your style or your strategy.

STUDY EXCELLENCE

One of the great things about becoming a serious writer is that you become a very serious reader. Every book you read from now on will have lessons for you; every facet of that book will have heightened resonance for you. Reading will still be an enjoyable entertainment, but it will be more than that.

Every author will be a tutor, every story a guide for your own work. This is not to say that you should copy other writers, though actually of course you should. Sometimes writers say that they don't read while they are writing in case another writer's style rubs off on them, but that, surely, would seem to be the point. Knowing all you can about your chosen craft gives you more options in your own writing.

Guitarists watch the hands of other players in order to spot new chord shapes and tricks of technique. Artists can become incredibly learned about the techniques of creating colour by looking at the painters of the eighteenth century. You should stay open-minded to writers whose taste is not your own, whose politics are not your own, whose subject matter you might find distasteful. You don't need to be a lesbian to enjoy the strong characters, heady atmospherics and powerfully plotted novels of Sarah Waters, for example.

You should also read contemporary work wherever possible. The world has moved on since the books you studied in high school. If you are serious about writing, you need to know what is happening now, as well as the masters of the past. Literature is a fashion-conscious business just like any other, and tastes change.

Everyone should have read *Treasure Island* at least three times, just as everyone should read Raymond Carver, Charles Dickens, Edgar Allan Poe, J. D. Salinger, Graham Greene, Jane Austen, P. D. James, George MacDonald Fraser's Flashman stories and F. Scott Fitzgerald. But you should also read E. L. Doctorow, A. L. Kennedy, Suzanne Berne, Don DeLillo, Anne Tyler, Deborah Levy, Sarah Hall, D.B.C. Pierre, Martin Amis and Monica Ali. All these modern novelists are very different in approach, and all master storytellers as well as great stylists. Keep an eye on the present, weigh up the competition and remember not to be depressed by great writing – just reading it with attention is building up your own literary muscle – but remember, too, that thinking you could do better is also a legitimate motivation for your own work.

The enemies of good style

CLICHÉ

A cliché is a phrase that has become stale with overuse: 'weak at the knees', 'over the moon', 'white as a sheet'. As *Fowler's Modern English Usage* reminds us, the word 'cliché' has 'come to be applied to commonplace things of other kinds – visual images, stock situations, remarks in radio and television ("And now, if you'll excuse me, I've got work to do"), ideas and attitudes, etc.'

You should also avoid clichéd situations: the husband who arrives home from work unexpectedly to find his wife in the arms of another man; or the suicide note on the mantelpiece. Dianne Doubtfire put it well when she said, 'Good style has a lot to do with freshness of vision.' My personal pet hate among clichés is where someone seems to vomit noisily as they come across a dead body. I'm sure this happens sometimes, but in literature, theatre and television it happens all the time and in the same kinds of ways.

Write out clichés

Make a list of all the clichés you can think of off the top of your head. Write a short story that includes as many of them as possible. Now rewrite the story, but find fresh, imaginative alternatives for all the stale old phrases.

SENTIMENTALITY

This is normally caused by overwriting a powerful scene involving a character you care for. It's easily done when that character is facing a moment of acute crisis. Read these passages with a stony heart, and be particularly receptive to criticisms that any early readers may have about these passages. As Carl Jung put it, 'Sentimentality is a superstructure covering brutality.'

CLUMSY PHRASES

These are phrases that can jerk readers from the world you are constructing for them into the real world. Something irritates. Reading out loud any phrases you suspect might be awkward will be the final test. Speaking the words out loud will also help you find your way to a better way of putting things.

TOO MANY ADJECTIVES AND ADVERBS

The most common but most easily corrected of all the mistakes that beginners make is to overuse adjectives and adverbs. Adverbs also tend to be the mark of lazy writing, telling us what someone thinks or feels rather than showing us. Adjectives have a dulling effect on a piece of prose, limiting the reader's own imagination and suggesting a lack of confidence on the part of the writer.

It engenders a feeling that they can't quite manage to describe a person or event properly. It makes readers feel that they are not in safe hands: that the pilot doesn't quite know how to fly the plane.

Focus point

Getting rid of as many adverbs as you can when revising a piece of work will be the simplest way to improve it.

Write a piece

Write a descriptive piece of 300 words or so, using no adjectives or adverbs. When the work is finished you may add one of each.

Edit the piece

Now imagine that you have been asked to turn that 300-word description into a 200-word piece for an anthology of new writing.

POOR PUNCTUATION

It's not really the role of this book to teach you about punctuation – for that you need Lynne Truss's excellent *Eats, Shoots & Leaves* – but be aware that editors will not correct incoherent grammar or punctuation; they will merely assume that you don't know what you're doing. In particular, be careful to use colons and semicolons correctly.

The other important point to make about punctuation (which is also actually a style point) is to refrain from using exclamation marks. It is like adding boom-boom after a joke. It's OK if you're Basil Brush but unacceptable otherwise.

Your punctuation and spelling

Contrary to popular opinion, publishers still expect their writers to be able to sort out their own punctuation and spelling. They won't have anyone who will do it for you. If your manuscript suggests that its writer is illiterate, it will go in the bin.

Monique Roffey

'When you come to do a second draft, that's the time to ask yourself if the narrative devices you've chosen, perhaps instinctively, are the right ones to use – tense, point of view, systems of images, metaphors and language too. Are these devices working, and have you been consistent? These are the big questions to consider once the first draft is over. After that, take a week off to sit in bed with jugs of coffee and READ the manuscript; by that I mean skim-read at least twice – for a bird's-eye view of the plot and the overall structure.

'Once you are happy you are telling the story in the right way, read the whole thing much more carefully – and start to make notes for changes and cuts. Once that is done, apply notes.'

(Monique Roffey is the author of Sun Dog (Scribner).)

Where to next?

Revising your work is vital, no matter what form you're working in. Be ruthless. You won't regret it. Bear this in mind as we move on to look at other forms of writing – stage plays, radio plays and screenwriting – in the coming chapters.

12

Writing stage plays

The theatre can be a hugely exciting medium. It is, after all, one of the few experiences that can't be downloaded. In live performance, there is always a sense of danger present, an immediacy that can't be found anywhere else. When great actors are performing great work, directed imaginatively on a stunning set, there is simply nothing else that can exhilarate in quite the same way.

The theatre today is throwing up some of the most provocative, challenging and mesmerizing work. The first thing a prospective theatre writer must do, therefore, is get out there and see some new plays. In this chapter you will learn about the key elements of a play: an inciting incident, action and conflict. You'll find out the best ways to create characters for the stage, how to structure a play and how to write stage dialogue. You'll also learn how to market a play.

The purpose of theatre

The play is increasingly becoming a marginal art form. Fewer and fewer people go and see plays and hardly anyone at all is brave enough to go and see a new play by a new writer with an unknown lead. When was the last time you went to see one?

The reasons are not hard to find. Plays are expensive. It can cost £20 ($30) or more for a ticket, so with drinks, programmes, a meal out and a babysitter an average couple can have spent a substantial amount to spend two hours trapped in a stuffy black box with no escape route should the play not prove to their taste. It's a hard expense to justify – even for the most dedicated lover of the arts. And yet … and yet … the theatre continues to survive and to throw up some outstanding, incredible work. Some of it even makes money occasionally.

Iain Crichton Smith

'This is what I tell them about drama. A stranger comes to the door And the arranged plates fall off the walls.'
('Drama Workshop')

A good night at the theatre has some of the thrill of attending a top live sporting event. It is an experience that is individual – we all experience the ideas and action of the play in our own way – but it is also communal. All of us in the audience have come together to share our common humanity. Part of us is lost to the crowd. An audience has its own dynamic, which is greater than, and different from, all the individuals in it. It is an intimate, very powerful place to be.

Make notes on the plays you see

Make four columns. In the first write a list of the last five plays you went to see and the rough dates. In the second give them a star rating out of five. Five stars for amazing, one for unwatchable. (Writers, directors and actors hate the star rating system adopted by most reviewers, mainly because it is all readers of reviews look at. Their frustration is understandable. Nevertheless, it is a very useful shorthand guide for audiences.) In the third column, write a couple of words or a sentence saying why you went to the show. If it was because of a star name, write 'star', if it was because of a review, put that down. If it was because a friend told you it was good, put that down. In the final column write down one thing that stood out from the play. If it was a line or a speech, then jot that down, but it might also be the set, the costumes or just one piece of action that stayed with you.

At the end of this exercise you should have a clear idea of how hard it is to get people to the theatre, what does attract them and also that what captures the imagination is not necessarily the words.

It should also be clear to you that, if you haven't seen a good play in a while, then you need to get out more. Don't rely on what you remember from school visits long ago. Find the listings pages in your local paper or on the web and book some tickets. Most theatres now have special deals available for those who book early or who book several shows at once, or who will see the matinee or who are prepared to go on unpopular nights and sit in the cheapest seats.

Stage characters

Characters are vital in a play. They can be extreme, but they should be three-dimensional. They should have vitality and they should not be your ciphers. They should think, breathe, walk and talk for themselves. Yes, you gave them life but you shouldn't think that gives you the right to push them around and tell them what to do, any more than you can completely control the lives of your children or friends.

You may not be able to control the directions in which your characters move or the places where they lead you, but you will still need to know everything about them. This includes where they went to school, their first romances, their job, what they like for breakfast, whether they prefer coffee to tea. Everything. Your audience doesn't need to know all this, but you do.

We've already done a lot of work on finding characters and you should have a little store built up and developed from those that you see around you every day, or that you used to know well. These people, with a little imaginative work, could change from ordinary real-life workmates, family, friends and acquaintances into characters given life by you.

What you should not do is create a character who is too obviously heroic – a kind of superman. They won't be believable. They may even be ridiculous and that ridiculousness will be heightened if they are the character that is meant to be most like you.

Real human beings

Your characters should be real, flawed human beings. And that remains true if your subject is Mother Teresa, Pope John Paul II or Gandhi – perhaps even more so.

Create characters

Choose three characters for this exercise: make one older and one younger and the third whatever age you want. It doesn't matter what sex they are. Make sure you give each of them a name; names are very important. It is hard to make a character come alive until you've found the right name for them.

Set your clock, watch or phone for 15 minutes and simply brainstorm as many questions as you can that you might want to ask your characters. These might range from 'What is your address?' all the way to 'Do you believe in God?'

Now spend some more thoughtful time making sure that you get all your characters' answers to the questions. At the end of this exercise you should have a more complete idea of what makes them tick. You should know them better as complex, fully rounded human beings.

A small cast

Small casts are a good idea. You don't need many characters for a decent play. These days, with the economics of the business being what they are, the fewer actors a producer needs to employ, the more interest they may have in reading your piece.

It is helpful if your characters are very different from one another. Now you need to find a reason for your characters to meet and begin their journey together. You need an inciting incident.

The inciting incident

This is the thing that kicks off the play, the thing that brings your characters together. It is some kind of event. And it is striking how often in plays this is actually the aftermath of something major. *Macbeth* starts just after the battle where Macbeth and King Duncan have seen off the rebel Macdonald and his Norwegian allies; *Hamlet* begins just after the marriage between Hamlet's mother and his dead father's brother; *Twelfth Night* begins after a storm has shipwrecked Viola and her twin brother. And so on.

This convention is not, of course, restricted to Shakespeare. Modern dramatists generally stick with it. Whether it's as dramatic as the death that has brought three estranged sisters together (*Memory of Water*) or as simple as an eviction requiring that a mother and her daughter find new lodgings (*A Taste of Honey*), often the inciting incident has happened just before the play begins and the characters are trying, in their different ways, to cope with the fallout from that.

Don't feel that you have to be too dark or too serious in these opening moments of a play. Humour is one of the key things that makes us warm to the characters. We need to be engaged by them if we are going to stay in their company for the next couple of hours. Plays often start with a moment of a release. Even if the event that has brought the characters together is a funeral, there is often laughter.

Write a scenario

Choose one of the following scenarios:

A It is the sixteenth birthday of one of your characters. To celebrate, they bought a lottery scratchcard and have won a large sum of money. On the way home they meet someone else.

B One of your characters knew one of the others a long time ago. They meet by chance on a bus.

C An elderly person is having trouble coping on their own and someone they know has decided it is time for them to move into sheltered accommodation.

D Someone has been offered a new job, which means moving away. The character breaks the news to someone close to them.

You can use characters you came up with earlier or invent new ones. Write 50 words or so about how the conversation might go. What might the characters want to get out of the conversation?

In order to do this exercise well it is very important to think about status and conflict.

Status

Everyone suffers from some kind of status anxiety at least some of the time. Some people suffer from it nearly all the time. Where do I fit into the world? Are my friends doing better than me? Where am I in the pecking order?

One of the mistakes King Lear makes is to think that his status will survive his giving over some of his royal powers to his daughters. Your characters will want to maintain or improve their status in the face of the pressures and temptations you give them. It is possible, of course, to have an apparently low-status role but to actually be high status in a particular situation. We all know firms where the cleaners or receptionists seem to have higher status than the bosses; shops where customers about to spend a great deal of money on designer clothes seem to have lower status than the teenage shop assistant serving them; and we all know households where the smallest child seems to rule the roost.

Conflict

Conflict is at the heart of all drama. It doesn't mean violence, fights
and arguments (though it might mean all of these), but it does mean
that characters must clash. Of course, the differing status of your
characters may mean that they are not all equally free to express
how they feel. A frustrated low-level employee may have to use
subtle means to get across their true feelings towards a bullying
boss. A shy daughter may have her own methods of conducting a
rebellion against what she sees as the harsh rule of a mother.

Of course, the responses of your characters may not be verbal. Plays
are about action, not words.

Write a scene

1 Script a short scene between the two characters you used in
  the last exercise, making sure that first you have given each
  one a status level out of ten (ten being high and one very low).
  As you write your script, remember that we rarely discuss
  the perceived status of one another. In conversation, we try
  to maintain the fiction that everybody is equal, though we all
  usually know that there are certain people whose feathers we try
  not to ruffle because of their power over us, or because of their
  worries and insecurities about status.

2 Now repeat the exercise but reversing the status levels.

It is interesting how your characters' efforts to get what they want from a meeting or a conversation are limited by their status. It is interesting, too, how having a secret can raise or lower a character's status or make them more vulnerable to changes in their status as the scene progresses.

Rewrite the scene

Now rewrite the scene but this time the characters' status must swap over gradually. Your nine must become your one and vice versa. Without being too clumsy or too obvious, you need to develop this meeting so that the top dog loses power to the underdog. Aim to do this over two pages of script.

Setting out your script

New writers for the stage often worry too much about the layout of the script. A good producer, director or actor will see quality however it is presented. But that is no reason to make it harder for them than it has to be.

Briefly, you need to set out your script like this:

First page – top right, header with draft number, name of play and author

Second page – cast list

Third page – Act One, centred

Fourth page – Scene One, underlined

Only use brackets for stage directions and keep the directions in capitals or italics.

Have your characters' names in bold on the left and your dialogue clearly separated.

There are software programs such as Final Draft that will do all this for you and, if you are wanting to go on and write more plays, or write for radio or television, then it is probably worth considering investing in one of these.

Tension

Audiences want to care for the characters and they want to worry about them. Your characters should be under some kind of threat or face some kind of choice. How they deal with that threat, or the consequences of their choices, is what provides the tension. They also have to respond to the actions and choices of others. There may be shifting alliances and power plays between the characters.

Remember that changes in characters happen gradually and the fact that you only have an hour or so to make big changes happen means you have to use even more subtlety so that audiences don' t think the change is rushed or forced. You have to give proper amounts of time for people to grow and transform. Arguments should heat up slowly and revelations should be drip-fed. Secrets may burst from a character in a sudden rush but there will usually have been clues in their demeanour or body language to the burdens that they have been carrying.

In the previous exercises, you dealt with issues of conflict and status between two characters. It will be interesting to see what happens when you add a third issue.

Add a third character

Look back at the exercises above for two characters, and try to take your scene further with the entrance of a third character. Decide in advance what your third character wants from the scene and what their status is in relation to the others. Now you have a situation where three agendas are competing. Aim to add at least another two pages to your script.

Dialogue versus action

As in novels, the speech in plays is not the same as speech in real life, though we often pretend that it is. What you are trying to do is distil the essence of real life and to create believable dialogue that also advances the story you want to tell. The words should sound natural to those characters in that particular situation. And be aware, too, that your characters will use different words depending on their age, background and education. Some will be more articulate than others. Some will grow more articulate as a scene develops or as their passion about a subject increases. For some, passion will rob them of their usual fluency. It's up to you to make these decisions. And, once again, remember that actions are the key to successful drama, not simply the words.

Eleanor Moran

'Dialogue is as much about what your character doesn't say as what they do. You must think about how they express themselves in a way that is unique to them.'

(Eleanor Moran is the author of Stick or Twist (Michael Joseph).)

Focus point

Read your lines out loud. This is good practice for all writers but it is especially important for theatre writers. It is only through hearing your characters speak that you can hear the bum notes, the clunky lines. It's even better if you can rope in some competent readers to voice the different parts.

One great modern playwright, Tim Fountain, once said, 'The words in a play are to give the actors something to do, not something to say.' Plays are about characters' actions, not their words. In fact, the words of a character might well be part of an attempt to disguise their actions. This gives the audience that complicated pleasure known as dramatic irony, by which they know more than the characters do.

If it is to work, your play should be full of action. I don't mean that it should have car chases and sword fights and explosions. It should have the more powerful action of human beings striving to achieve their goals, of trying to balance contradictory impulses.

Not a lot needs to happen in your play, however, for it to be chock-full of action and incident. It's just that those events that *are* there must be full of meaning and significance for the characters in the play. For example, if a downtrodden wife places a cup a centimetre out of reach of her dictatorial husband when usually she hands it to him directly, this may tell us about the beginnings of a revolt against tyranny. Subtle shifts of power can also be detected by an audience in a squabble about who is paying for the coffee. Each scene of your play is going to see the characters groping towards desires that might be obvious to the audience, but not to the other characters and maybe not even to themselves.

Real life distilled

Drama is distilled real life, not real life itself, so each word, each line, must be in the script for a purpose. It must move the action along in some way. It must justify itself. Don't use speeches to reveal character. Use action to show character instead. The words characters speak should be there because they have to be there. They are things that the characters have to say.

Structure

The key to being a good playwright is right there, in the name, playwright. First of all, it is play. It should be fun. No one wants to go to the theatre to be lectured at. We get enough of that at home, at work, at school. We might hope to learn things from the show but we don't want to notice that we are being taught. And you need to bring a sense of fun and mischief to your drama if you want it to work. Humour is one of the best ways to get an audience caring about your characters right at the start. And we need to care, even about the characters we learn to despise later. We need to feel involved in them and their struggles, desires and dilemmas.

Shaping and crafting

Plays are constructed as much as they are written. Again, the clue is there in the job title. Playwrights are, like wheelwrights and shipwrights, makers of physical entities. If you can think of your play as a physical thing that needs shaping and crafting, then you are likely to be more successful than if you just pour your heart out on to the page.

Write in scenes

This seems obvious. It's a play: of course, it will be in scenes. But what we really mean is that each scene should have a rhythm and momentum of its own. As well as staging posts on the way to the final resolution of the piece, they should be complete in themselves with their own tensions, secrets, desires and resolutions. Each scene is like a play in itself, one that also advances the plot and action of the work as a whole.

Keep your scenes tight in terms of space and time. Audiences often find very short scenes and large gaps in time very off-putting in a theatrical context.

Workshop exercise

Look at the scene you have written and think about the following questions.

- Take each of your characters in turn. What is the journey that each one of them makes? How are they going to be changed by the events that take place? Write out an arc for each of them.
- Do all of your characters suffer some ups and downs as the play progresses? Make sure each character has an interesting ride.
- Now try to break that story into five further scenes. Make notes about what will happen in each scene.
- Ask yourself whether each scene has its own beginning, middle and end. Every scene should be like a play in itself.
- Each scene should also reveal a bit more of the various stories of your three characters as they intersect with one another. What do we know about the characters now that we didn't at the beginning? How do these revelations affect the other characters' journeys?

A singular setting

Many plays that have continued pleasing audiences for years, decades or longer have taken place in one unchanging setting. Often this can be one room: for example, one of the authors of this book has had a play produced that took place entirely in the rehearsal room of a small-time rock band and another one set solely in a girl's bedroom.

Multiple locations and sudden shifts between them – that work in film – can be jarring for a theatre audience and hard to pull off on stage. As you become more experienced, you will find ways of getting around this problem; for now, however, you will find it easier to restrict your characters' movements. Many great plays have been set in one room. Think of Arthur Miller's *The Crucible*, where the action takes place largely in the courthouse, the plays of Oscar Wilde, which are mostly set in drawing rooms over tea, or those of Samuel Beckett where characters hardly move from one spot.

It was the ancient Greeks who first came up with the rules that have for thousands of years governed the way that theatre works. Obviously, these have been meddled with and experimented with many times over the centuries but still audiences respond best to a play that respects what Aristotle called the unities of Time, Place and Action. People still mostly like a play that begins at the beginning and moves in a linear fashion to a conclusion.

Lastly, theatre seems to be the place where our common humanity can be best played out. It is a more intimate, more shared experience than any other art form. Stories, novels and poems are often private communions between writer and reader, while films are often huge spectacles removed from our everyday experience by the sheer size of the screen as well as by the Hollywood subject matter. Television often has the opposite effect. We watch actors and stories shrink to a less-than-human size and we watch them in our private or family spaces. It is only really stage drama that gives us a sense of ourselves. Crammed together in the dark watching living, breathing people a few feet away grappling with the pain of living ... What could be more life-affirming than that? Even if it has cost us a fortune in babysitters and overpriced Merlot.

Write a short play

Write a short play for your three characters. Aim for between 10 and 15 minutes (or about ten pages). Each character should be changed by the end of your play and the status that they began with altered, too.

How to market your play

Theatres often have a literary manager whose job it is to read new scripts with a view to possible performance. The more conscientious or progressive theatres will ensure that they give detailed feedback on scripts, though you may have to wait a while as they get dozens of scripts every single week.

In addition, many theatres have a playwrights' group where you can meet other writers and discuss your work. These theatres may also run a programme offering new writers the opportunity to have their work read or workshopped, and these can be very useful places to start. The theatres that have these programmes will very often have one-act play festivals to which you can submit work. You should see whether there is a local theatre with a scheme like this. If nothing else, it is very often a chance to meet theatre professionals and find out what is currently exciting them. Other theatres will run competitions to which new writers can submit work, and often theatres will follow up promising writers, even if they don't use the particular play that was submitted.

Many regions of the UK and most districts of the United States have thriving playwright networks that offer mutual support to emerging writers. Touring companies are also often on the lookout for exciting new work. Try to find out about as many of these as you can: see their shows. Since the decline of the old rep theatres (many of which nonetheless defy the odds and cling on), the touring theatre companies have become the place where a lot of important theatre professionals learn their craft. This includes actors, directors and producers as well as writers. Many of these companies are small outfits formed by actors just out of drama school, attempting to generate their own work so as not to be reliant simply on the vagaries of the job market. A lot of these companies will be interested in reading scripts that the bigger theatres just won't want to take a chance on.

Another thing worth doing is to try to get a director who will champion your work. It is often easier to get a director on board than a theatre – there are a lot more of them for a start and they are also looking for work that excites them.

Another route to try is drama schools, which are often looking for scripts that will challenge their students, or amateur companies which, at the very least, might be willing to give your play a rehearsed reading.

Focus point

If you are going to have actors speak your words, you should try to get a feel for the job they do. Join a theatre group and get used to the difficulties of playing a part. You needn't be an actor, but become involved somehow. You can stage-manage, build sets or sell tickets, but you should try to be around plays as they are put together. You should try to develop a feel for the mechanics of them.

Adaptation

Adapting a novel or, as is becoming increasingly common, a film for the stage can be a useful way into writing for the theatre. Audiences – and producers – often like to minimize the risks involved in a night at the theatre by ensuring that they already know the story, or at least that the story is one which has already stood the test of time. It means that you don't have to worry so much about creating character or plot. That's already done for you, though deciding what to cut while retaining the essential vitality of the original is a special surgical skill of its own.

A good way of beginning an adaptation without getting bogged down in the minutiae of a novel's plots and subplots is to read the original (or watch the film) carefully twice and then put it aside and write out a three-page synopsis. What you have kept in is probably the heart of the story – or, at least, those aspects of the story that engage you most directly.

🔑 Choosing what to adapt

If you choose to adapt a well-loved piece, expect to take some flak from its devotees. It might be more interesting for you as a writer to find a work that hasn't been done too often – something unusual, or a forgotten or neglected classic.

💬 Willy Russell

'When writing a play, the most important thing is to do it – not talk about doing it, intend to do it, mean to do it, plan to do it or dream of doing it. Do it. The world is full of those who talk about doing it, dream, mean, intend, plan to do it – when they find the right time or the right place or the right computer, the right pen, the right paper, the right frame of mind. The writer knows that there is no right this or right that and to write a play (or indeed anything else) you have to DO IT. Good luck.'

(Willy Russell is the author of many successful stage plays including Blood Brothers, Educating Rita *and* Shirley Valentine *(all Heinemann).)*

Where to next?

There's something magical about seeing the world you created in your head brought to life by talented actors. In the next few chapters we're going to look at writing other kinds of scripts, first for radio and then for television and film.

13

Writing radio plays

Writing radio drama has been a springboard for many great writers, while those who have made their name in other areas, such as film or theatre or poetry, still like to return to writing for radio because of some of the special benefits it offers. This doesn't mean that it is an easy medium. The rules of drama still apply and your words must be even better because your words are what will sustain an audience's interest.

This chapter explains how to overcome the obstacles of the medium and produce a worthwhile piece of radio writing. It covers the importance of thinking visually and how to use sound and music. It examines the advantages of using a narrator and directly addressing the audience. Finally, there is advice on where to send your radio play.

The BBC

One of the things that is great about the UK is the BBC. It might not feel like it sometimes as we are bullied into going digital whether we want to or not, and when we find that, despite an ever-increasing licence fee, there seems to be nothing on television but talent contests, quizzes and reality shows. Nevertheless, a state-funded (but not state-controlled) television and radio service dedicated to entertaining and informing without necessarily worrying about commercial interests or ratings is a rare privilege and the envy of the entire developed world. And one of the glories of the BBC is the continuing interest in radio drama.

Nowhere else in the world is as much effort put into radio plays. BBC radio creates high-quality drama featuring some of the world's best-known actors and brightest writing stars every single day. The production values on BBC radio drama are incredibly high and the range of styles and subjects is immense. Of course, not all the dramas broadcast on BBC Radio 3 and 4 are produced in-house. There are many smaller production companies that produce work commissioned by the BBC. And there are other networks that produce radio drama, though not in the same quantity as the Beeb.

Writers in the United States and other countries do not have the same access to radio plays (though NPR in the States produces some). Writers from other countries are, however, not barred from writing for the UK market. And, with the advent of the Internet, the output of the BBC is available to anyone who cares to listen. A little bit of time and trouble and the American, Australian or, indeed, Siberian writer, can listen to the BBC's high-quality radio drama and get a feel for this exciting medium.

Steve Allen

'Radio is the theatre of the mind; television is the theatre of the mindless.'

Liberation

Most theatre or even film directors would blanch at the idea of a story that takes place in outer space, features talking dolphins and travels through many centuries in time. Yet in radio all of this is possible. It is even, in the case of *The Hitchhiker's Guide to the Galaxy* (which began life as a series on BBC Radio 4), possible within the same piece of work. By using sound to unlock the listener's imagination there is no setting that need be ruled out on grounds of cost or practicality. If your play features two pit ponies conducting a love affair down a mineshaft in the early years of the seventeenth century, this is entirely feasible.

A writer for radio has the freedom to write about any subject, any idea and set their story in any time in history including the distant future. You can write about real figures, without worrying about getting an actor who looks like the historical character. You can also write in several lengths. There are slots for 30-minute, 45-minute, 60-minute and 90-minute plays. And then there are dramas in several parts.

A liberating medium

A writer for radio is released from a lot of the usual constraints that inhibit the stage dramatist. Radio can be the most liberating medium of all.

While writing drama for radio may be liberating in many ways, the rules of drama – engaging characters, conflict, narrative drive, tension, vivid, believable dialogue, an awareness of status – still apply. Your words need to do all this work because, despite all the other things that a skilled radio producer and director can bring to the piece, it is essentially your words that will hold an audience's interest. And there are some major additional obstacles to overcome to produce a worthwhile piece of radio writing.

The vision thing

The radio dramatist is utilizing the most powerful tool a writer can have: the imagination of the audience. We've discussed elsewhere the fact that audiences like to work; they like to become actively engaged with the action no matter what medium the story is told in. In radio the writer's chief skill lies in helping the audience to picture the setting, characters and events. This means that the language of the play can be heightened. Whereas in stage drama a lot can be gauged through action and gesture, on radio the language has to carry a lot more of the weight. This is why it can be such a great medium for poets who are already used to writing in images. You have to create a vivid image in the listener's mind from sound alone, and though there is a lot that can be done with sound effects, still the writer is going to have to ensure that there is enough visual detail in the words for the listener's imagination to feed on.

Focus point

The paramountcy of words in radio drama doesn't mean that the writer needs to use lots of adjectives. Don't have your characters mention the 'vast blue sky' or similar clichés, but you should at least think about colour and description in your dialogue.

Describe a scene

Look out of the window nearest to your writing desk. Take a mental photograph. Now move away from the scene – turn your back if you have to – and write a detailed description in such a way that a reader or a listener could picture it exactly. Aim for 100 words. After you have done this, look again. What have you missed out?

Now, imagine that some kind of crime has taken place outside your window. It can be minor or serious. Then, imagine that a patient, experienced policeman is trying to coax a description of the offence from a witness.

This simple exercise gives you an inciting incident, two strong characters in the policeman and the witness, some tension as the witness describes the event and some human engagement (because we can all sympathize with the victims of crime and empathize with the situation of both the witness and the copper). However, it also tests your power to create pictures inside a listener's head.

Direct address

One of the chief pleasures of writing for radio is that you can use direct address. This simply means a character telling a story directly to the audience. It can be a powerful tool on the stage, too, but writers (and audiences) are nervous of it because it seems to disturb the illusion in which we are unseen, unnoticed spectators as events unfold on stage. Theatre folk often talk about the 'fourth wall', meaning the imaginary, invisible barrier that divides the audience from the actors (the other three walls being those at the side and behind the stage). The idea that someone can talk through this wall directly to the audience can still seem disturbing and dangerously experimental to some people.

In radio, by contrast, it is almost essential. In radio a character speaking thoughts out loud in a stream of consciousness is a completely valid, universally accepted device. It is because of this that radio is the natural place for those who love the idea of writing monologues.

The power of direct address

Characters talking from the heart about their innermost feelings and key memories, and doing it directly into the head of the listener, is one of the most powerful and intimate exchanges that writers can have with their audience.

Write a monologue

Write a short monologue about a key memory from your past. Perhaps you have a secret or something that you have told only a very few people. Try to choose something that you think has shaped the person you have become now. Don't worry about how personal it is or how upsetting. In any case, no one but you has to read it. You can always destroy your writing as soon as you have completed this exercise. I bet you don't, though.

Remember Hemingway's advice to a writer: 'Write hard about what hurts.' In the end, what was painful or hurtful to us becomes material that we can process for the entertainment and enlightenment of others. One of the joys of being a writer is that we can use the hurt of the past to bring complicated but lasting pleasure into the present.

Using a narrator

Using a narrator in radio drama is very useful as a device for moving the listener between scenes. The narrator can also become a way of turning the stage directions into part of the action and for describing the passage of time.

Write three short scenes

1. Write two short scenes. The first is between a young boy and his mother. The boy is five years old and it is his first day of school. He is seeking to reassure his anxious mother that he will be all right.

2. The second scene takes place 13 years later. The boy is now 18 years old and about to leave home to go to university. The conversation mirrors the first one, though of course it will have some key differences as the boy is now grown up.

3. Now write a third scene, where either the mother or the son describes in a few sentences what has happened to the two of them in the years between the two scenes. You can make this linking scene more powerful by addressing it to the person who isn't narrating. In other words, the mother will address the son as 'you' or vice versa.

Putting the listener in the position of a person being talked to is also more effective on radio than in the theatre. In the theatre we are always slightly conscious of all the other people around us, so when a character addresses us as 'you' the intimacy is never entirely convincing. On radio, because we are usually listening on our own, it is easier to be drawn into the illusion of identifying with the person being talked to.

Including sound

It may seem obvious, but as a radio writer you will need to be thinking constantly about sound in the same way that a stage writer must always be thinking about action. You should be meticulous in making sure that your scripts are full of sounds that tell the reader where they are and what is happening.

Music

Music is evocative in all forms of drama, but for radio writers it is an essential way to develop moods. Songs can place your audience immediately in a particular place and time. Music can act as an extremely effective form of shorthand, a great way to set a scene without the need for dialogue explaining where the characters are. It was Noël Coward who coined the line about 'the potency of cheap music' (and he should know), and it is true that popular music can add a great deal of resonance to a piece.

Fashions in music tend to come in waves. Rock and roll burst on to the cultural scene in the middle of the 1950s. The Beatles changed everything again in the early 1960s. Glam, progressive rock, heavy metal, disco and punk all staked their claims in the 1970s, while the 1980s saw the dominance of synthesizer bands and the New Romantics as well as the birth of hip-hop and rap.

From 'Rock around the Clock' up to the recent hits by the Arctic Monkeys and others, pop music has soundtracked the lives of generations of teenagers. It might be that the very ubiquity of popular music has now diluted its impact, but for the radio writer songs can still help set the tone, and even help tell the story of a piece. They don't do this in the obvious way that the songs in a musical do, but the songs of a period can provide a sly subplot of their own that gives support or contrast to the main action.

Choose your key songs

Choose three or four key moments in your life that you think you might like to write about one day. Now write down the songs that were important at these times. They can be those that had special significance for you personally (perhaps they were songs you had played at your wedding or at a family funeral?) or they can simply be whatever was in the charts or on the radio at the time.

The sound of silence

In a stage drama, silence can be very powerful. It gives the audience a chance to focus on the body language of the actors. Their gestures, movements, facial expressions, the way they handle the props, all of these can be revealing. Some of the most powerful scenes ever performed achieved their impact through the agonizing gaps between the words. Beckett and Pinter are the acknowledged masters of the art of silence, but there are others, too.

In radio it is also possible to use silence well. However, if the pause goes on for more than a couple of seconds your listeners may assume that there has been a power cut and will start fiddling with the dials. This is the last thing you want. Using silence in radio drama is like using a rare and precious spice in cooking – the finest saffron, say – so you want to be careful not to waste it.

Workshop exercise

In this workshop we're going to look again at the short stage play you wrote in the previous chapter. The following questions should help you think about how that play could make the transition from stage to radio:

1. Let's start with sound. Where is your play set? Make a list of all the sound effects you would need to conjure up that environment in the minds of your listeners. It might be the shuffle-thunk of an office photocopier, the distant cries of herring gull, the chatter and clatter of a busy café. Don't forget about music – which songs provide the soundtrack to your characters' lives?

2. Look for visual details in your script that you could convey through dialogue. Are there any important objects or details that you would need to explain to a radio audience?

3. If your stage play contained a lot of action that might be lost on radio – elaborate physical comedy, for example – you might need to find another way to convey this. Could a funny incident be relayed as a comic monologue or through a conversation?

Where to send your radio script

The BBC has a number of initiatives designed to help new writers and writers wanting to work on radio drama in particular. Perhaps the best place to start is the Writers' Room: www.bbc.co.uk/writersroom.

The BBC is also involved in the Alfred Bradley Award, which is a competition run with the express purpose of finding new writers for radio. Each shortlisted entrant receives the chance to develop work for radio while the winner also gets £5,000 and their work broadcast. The competition is a great way to get your work noticed and gives you something to aim for. It is also judged by writers of a high calibre, so that you know your efforts are being read by the best of your peers.

Focus point

You should also be considering sending your work to producers whom you admire. If you are serious about writing for radio, you will be listening to a lot of plays and you will always find the name of the producer listed in the end credits, which will also tell you which studio the play was recorded in.

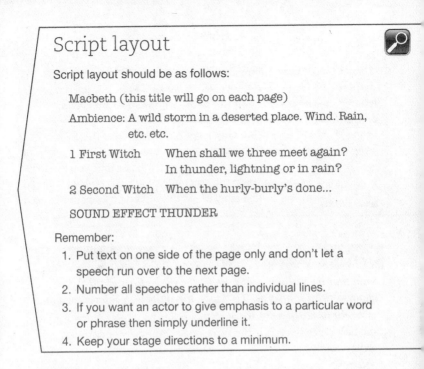

Script layout

Script layout should be as follows:

> Macbeth (this title will go on each page)
>
> Ambience: A wild storm in a deserted place. Wind. Rain, etc. etc.
>
> 1 First Witch   When shall we three meet again?
>   In thunder, lightning or in rain?
>
> 2 Second Witch   When the hurly-burly's done...
>
> SOUND EFFECT THUNDER

Remember:

1. Put text on one side of the page only and don't let a speech run over to the next page.
2. Number all speeches rather than individual lines.
3. If you want an actor to give emphasis to a particular word or phrase then simply underline it.
4. Keep your stage directions to a minimum.

Other radio outlets

Up to now we have focused largely on the BBC which, through Radio 3 and 4 and the World Service, produces the majority of radio drama in the UK. But there are other stations, particularly those that use the Internet as a way of broadcasting material. As audiences for niche programming and community-based stations grow, we may find that these become increasingly important outlets for drama.

Some leading radio writers

The work of those specializing in writing radio drama does not attract the attention given to writers in other media and it can be hard to find examples of their work. But you should try to track down plays by Lee Hall, Marcy Khan, Mike Walker, Mark Illis, Amanda Dalton and Nell Leyshon, all of whom have produced marvellous work for radio.

Mark Illis

'Over-formal, over-grammatical, on-the-nose dialogue will drain the life out of your writing. Make sure there's a subtext; remember how people tend not to answer questions directly – or at all; start the scene late and get out early. And dialogue is probably the easiest thing to overwrite, because it acquires its own momentum, so revise ruthlessly.'

(Mark Illis has written numerous radio plays that have been broadcast on BBC Radio 4. He also writes for film and television.)

Where to next?

Now that we've looked at writing for the radio and all the opportunities it affords, we'll take the skills we've developed and move on to writing for the screen.

14

Screenwriting

Screenwriting can, even now, be lucrative. An average television writer earns far more than all but the most famous and highly rewarded novelist. It is also a medium where talent, once spotted, can be promoted quickly into the mainstream.

In this chapter you will learn about writing for the range of basic television formats – serials, drama, sitcoms and soaps – and for film, and about the differences between the two media. There is information on how to begin writing collaboratively and how to structure and put together an outline and a script. You'll also find out where to send your outline and then your finished script as well as about opportunities for new screenwriters.

Why write for television?

The main attraction of writing for television is the potential for having your work seen by millions. It is also a medium that is voracious in its demand for stories. There are now hundreds of television channels that need to fill thousands of hours. Granted, a lot of those hours are taken up with talk shows, sport, adverts, old films, cartoons, reality shows, quizzes and reruns of past television shows – but there is still a large market hungry for fresh, innovative material.

Clive Barnes

'Television is the first truly democratic culture – the first culture available to everybody and entirely governed by what the people want. The most terrifying thing is what the people do want.'

The basic formats of television drama

THE CLOSED SERIAL

This is a story that comes to an end over several parts. The lengths of these dramas can vary. It is common to see two-part dramas where each part is an hour or two hours long. (These are often screened over two nights in the UK.) A story can also be told over six parts or more – in the form of a weekly serial. The benefit for writers of these longer serials is that they have time to develop character and drama in a more thorough way than would be possible in a programme shown over just a couple of nights. They have some of the novelist's luxury when it comes to taking time to move the story on.

The hope is that a weekly serial becomes a family event, where everyone sits down together at the same time each week to watch *Prime Suspect* or an Andrew Davies adaptation of a classic novel. Increasingly, however, technology means that these serials are not necessarily viewed at the same time each week but that people are watching at times which suit them. 'On demand' formats have put viewers very much more in charge of their television programming than ever before. Viewers can, in effect, create their own viewing schedules, which can make life difficult for television executives trying to tie an audience to a television 'appointment'. Also, viewers often now wait for the box set of a popular series to appear on DVD so that they can have the benefit of the reviews and the word of mouth about a programme before committing the time to watching it.

Social changes, too, have meant a corresponding change in television-watching habits. Many families have several televisions, so the chances of the whole family gathering together to watch the same show at the same time are increasingly unlikely. Nevertheless, this remains the holy grail of much television programming.

Focus point

A crossover show that appeals to parents, to young professionals and to at least older children is a show that is going to be talked about and attract advertisers.

THE ONE-HOUR DRAMA SERIES

This takes the form of a number of self-contained episodes. The plot will have its own three-act structure, but the characters will be the same week to week and will contain storylines that the audience are familiar with. Our enjoyment of the story will be enriched by our knowledge of the protagonists and the struggles they have outside the main plotline. One-hour drama series that work well are shows like *Without a Trace*.

THE SOAP

The soap is usually a half-hour open series that can be on several nights a week, featuring a cast of much-loved characters based around one central location such as Albert Square for *EastEnders* or Southfork ranch in *Dallas*. These can run for years and the storylines will reflect the dramas of ordinary life. They are intended to be realistic: a distillation of real life. Each soap will have started life with a 'Bible' that contains all the details of the characters and the locations.

Soaps are enormously popular but comparatively cheap to shoot and so can be the most effective kind of television drama. Soap operas and other long-term series use 'storyliners' to develop the plots, while writers are responsible for the dialogue and action of each individual episode. A typical soap opera might have up to 30 writers and half a dozen storyliners working on its production.

Write a scenario

This is a fun exercise that will get you in a soapy frame of mind. Get out a big piece of plain paper and draw a map of a village. It doesn't have to be a great cartographical achievement; just make sure there are plenty of houses. Now invent some people to live in the houses. Now invent some scandals for the people. Is the man who runs the post office having an affair with the vicar? Does the schoolteacher have something untoward buried under her patio? Have some fun and see just how intertwined you can make the lives of your villagers.

THE HALF-HOUR SITCOM

Television is always on the lookout for new comedy writing talent. It is also the area where there is most likely to be a level playing field. When it comes to writing comedy it either makes the audience laugh, in which case it is a success, or it doesn't, in which case it's a failure.

Focus point

For comedy, it doesn't matter who you know or if you've got a track record. If your script makes executives laugh, you are in with a shout of getting television to take a chance on you.

Situation comedies of the classic kind, like *Friends* and *I Love Lucy* in the United States or, in the UK, *Steptoe and Son*, *Are You Being Served?* and *The Likely Lads* – which have a few strong comic characters in one location – have rather fallen from favour in recent years and most comedies now seem to include a drama or soap opera element. The classic sitcom often seemed to be about class struggle. In *Steptoe and Son*, Harold Steptoe is forever trying to escape the role of rag-and-bone man and make something of himself, only to find his father continually bringing him down. In *Whatever Happened to the Likely Lads?*, Bob Ferris wants to leave behind the macho working-class culture he grew up with for a more bourgeois life with his posh new wife, but his childhood friend, the feckless Terry Collier, does everything he can to remind Bob of where he really belongs.

In the more modern sitcoms, focus has switched to struggles between the sexes rather than struggles over class identity. For example, *Men Behaving Badly* has the two male protagonists resisting growing up and settling down by any means necessary, while at the same time appeasing their long-suffering girlfriends.

In so far as it is possible to spot contemporary trends, many modern sitcoms seem to be about the battle of eccentric characters to maintain themselves within the confines of a conformist world. Think of *Green Wing* or *Black Books*. (This theme can also be detected in spoofs like *Life on Mars* where a modern, politically correct cop finds himself catapulted back in time to a rougher, more forthright world.)

In the United States, comedies like *Seinfeld* or *The Larry Sanders Show* differ in that they are built around characters who have worldly success, though they also have unlikeable and selfish traits. It is this self-obsession, a basic inability to empathize, that gets the characters into scrapes. Again, in a comedy like *The Office*, it is a character's self-delusion that provides the humour. He sees himself as a King of Comedy, the wit of his workplace, universally loved and admired, whereas in truth David Brent is unable to connect at an ordinary, functional level.

In general, popular American comedies tend to be more life-affirming and more obviously heart-warming. In *Seinfeld* the characters might lead gleefully empty lives (it is, after all, famously a 'show about nothing') but at least they are a supportive, close-knit unit. This is taken to a further extreme in *Friends*, where the whole premise is of a group ethos, where individual quirks are sublimated to a team ideal. The message of a sitcom like *Friends* is that we are greater together than we are alone – that whatever conflicts we have, they can be resolved by the intervention and love of our closest buddies.

This is also the message from influential comedies like *Cheers*, its spin-off, *Frasier*, and from shows like *Roseanne*. Individuals might fight, but in the end family or group loyalty will enable problems to be resolved. Even a character as ostensibly selfish as Larry David in *Curb Your Enthusiasm* is redeemed by his relationship with his long-suffering wife and with his old friends.

Remember, the boundaries between all these formats can seem blurred these days. Take *Shameless*, for example, or *Desperate Housewives*. Are these comedies, one-hour drama series or soaps? All three? It's hard to decide.

Where to start

If you feel that you can create strong characters, fast-moving plots and can write realistic, witty dialogue and, best of all, think visually, then it might be that television is the medium for you. And the best way to start is to write your own script. Don't write a version of one of the series or serials that are already out there. Try something completely new. Even if your dream is to write for *Coronation Street* or *Scrubs* eventually, don't start by writing a script for that show. Try something original. You'll have much more chance of impressing producers if you can come up with something where you have had to think of all the characters and stories yourself.

Structure

Whatever kind of television you want to write, you will need to conform to the structural rules of that format. The first thing to bear in mind is length. A half-hour programme is actually 23 minutes.

Similarly, an hour is 55 minutes. And these are inflexible rules. It's not like the theatre, where a piece can be roughly 90 minutes long. Television doesn't recognize rough lengths. Work on each page of your script being 40 seconds of airtime.

You should also adhere to the three-act structure of beginning, middle and end, with characters in jeopardy right from the start. This is true even if you are writing the first episode of what you hope will become a long-running show.

Rewrite a scene

Pick a scene you wrote in the last chapter and rewrite it as a television script. Read it out loud, leaving appropriate pauses for on-screen action. Time yourself, then try to edit the scene down so it lasts as close to 40 seconds as possible.

The outline

The first thing you need is an idea, a one-sentence concept that excites your imagination. You could begin with a simple 'What if …' What if you could meet your own 18-year-old self? Simple but exciting. Put your idea to a friend, or your writing partner if you have one (television writing is often done collaboratively – there is more about this later in the chapter). If they are sufficiently enthused, start putting together an outline immediately.

An outline is a short synopsis explaining the key characters and setting out the general plot. It needs to be written in as engaging a manner as possible. It should also be no more than two pages of double-spaced A4. The idea behind the outline is partly to give yourself a map through to the finished script, but also to intrigue potential producers enough so that they want to see the script. When you are an established television writer, it might be that this outline is all you need to get producers excited and they will commission a script (one which they will pay for) on the strength of this alone. Before you reach those heights, it will always be best to have an actual script to show.

Here is an example of the first paragraph of an outline for a new television show.

***Teenage Kicks* by M.I. and Stephen May**

The 18-year-old son you never knew you had shows up out of the blue. And he's embarrassing. He follows you around, heckling you all the time, because he thinks you've made too many compromises and wrong turnings. Why are you coming up with designs for sweet wrappers when you were going to be an artist? They call you Steady Eddie at work. What's that about? And you're getting married? Why?

Under that sort of pressure, you're bound to start questioning yourself. All right, this boy is immature. And naive. And yes, irritating and self-centred and obsessed by sex. But all the same — are you where you want to be? Have you made a grown-up, realistic accommodation with life, or have you just thrown away your dreams and buckled under?

But supposing your son does successfully pull the rug out from under you. Supposing you try to live the way he wants you to live. Is that likely to work out for a man who's knocking 40, with a mortgage and a fiancée?

Teenage Kicks suggests you might have something to learn from a younger, more idealistic voice. But it would be dangerous to get too carried away …

Write an outline

Write an outline for your favourite television show. Try to capture the essence of it in less than two pages.

After you have an outline, you can begin working on a scene breakdown. Scenes need to be short, probably far shorter than you realize. A one-hour television script may have 90 scenes or more. It will rarely have fewer than 70.

Your scene-by-scene breakdown may not contain absolutely every scene that goes into your eventual script but it is important that you have a step-by-step route plan to keep you focused on the story. Your characters will reveal themselves through their actions far more than through their dialogue. Remember that in television it is even more important that you show not tell. Television is a visual, technical medium where dialogue is always suppressed to make way for action. This is as true for comedy as it is for any other format, by the way.

Here is an example of the scene breakdown of the show which the outline came from:

7. INT. OFFICE/SARAH'S HOUSE

We see BARRY in action in the office. He's in a bad mood. He thought Eddie would be in early, today of all days. And why couldn't he get him on his mobile? A naked EDDIE claims he's on the bus, but BARRY is uninterested in EDDIE'S excuses. He's busy being vile to his staff KERRY, PAUL and JANICE. The call ends. The moment really has gone now. SARAH and EDDIE briefly reflect on what the promotion might mean. A new bathroom for one thing. EDDIE affects not to be too bothered. As long as that pushy young thing KERRY doesn't get it. 'You really don't like her do you?' SARAH is sympathetic and then reminds him that they have a dirty weekend away. Not too long to wait.

8. INT. OFFICE

9. SARAH'S HOUSE

A near-naked EDDIE watches from the window as ROB collects SARAH for her lift to school. He's irritated to see ROB give SARAH a social kiss on the cheek. EDDIE checks the time. Shit.

10. EXT. THE STREETS

EDDIE is running again. For the bus this time. We see the kid from scene 1 following him. He's not going to make the bus. As he gives up, the kid runs past him and makes the bus. EDDIE puts another spurt on but the doors close in his face.

11. INT. THE OFFICE

BARRY hires YOUNG EDDIE to replace the fired intern. YOUNG EDDIE wasn't really seeking employment but BARRY is hard to refuse. KERRY gives BARRY some lip. He doesn't like that.

Only when you have a very clear and detailed sense of your plot should you start on your script.

Write an outline and scenes

1. Write an outline for a television drama series based on a story you have written.
2. Now break the story down into scenes.

Layout

Remember to use Final Draft (www.finaldraft.com), or similar software, to make setting out your script as easy as possible and the finished product look professional. These are the basic rules:

- **Font**: Courier New 12.
- **Spacing**: single line spacing for action, character name and dialogue. Insert a double space between scene headings and action, and between scenes.
- **Page numbering**: top right.
- **Scene heading (aka the slug line)**: this is always in upper case, which makes it easy for production to count the number of times you use a particular location.
- **INT.** = interior or indoors: this is for any scene where characters are inside, whether it is a castle or a car.
- **EXT.** = exterior or outdoors: any scene where the characters are outdoors.
- **Action**: this is the 'business', i.e. what actually takes place in a scene. Keep it visual and concise. Your style describing scenes is an important part of the script – don't neglect it. Don't describe the characters' feelings or state of mind.
- **Characters' names**: capitalize so that those involved in production can see when a new character enters the action.
- **Dialogue**: indent with the character's name in capitals over the dialogue.
- **Sounds**: significant sounds are capitalized, e.g. SIRENS WAIL.
- **Parentheses**: use very occasionally to tell the producer or actor how a line is delivered. Don't use for action.

Here is an example of a television script layout:

```
INT. DESIGN REPUBLIC 09:36 THURS

EDDIE COMES INTO THE OFFICE. AS
THEY CLOCK HIM, EVERYONE BREAKS
UP FROM WHERE THEY ARE AND GETS
ON WITH THEIR WORK.
PAUL
What time do you call this?
EDDIE (SV)
Have I got the job? Have you
heard?
BARRY AND A SLIGHTLY TENSE KERRY
HAVE APPROACHED. KERRY IS 26,
TALENTED, SPARKY AND AMBITIOUS,
AND CLEARLY DOESN'T FIT IN AT
DESIGN REPUBLIC.
BARRY
I call it nine thirty six, which
makes you six minutes late.
EDDIE
Sorry, I know, but it's out of
character, you have to admit …
Hi, Kerry.
KERRY
Eddie.
EDDIE
All right?
KERRY
Fine.
BARRY
That's what I love about office
life, all the witty banter.
```

Note: SV = *sotto voce* – Latin for 'under one's breath'.

The calling card script

You need a script if you are going to have a career in writing for television. It's the only way anyone will tell whether you are any good. It should be as good and as polished a script as you can make it. The chances are that it will never be made but it should show you at your best. It is obviously in your best interests to show producers that you are not only a gifted writer but that you are professional and painstaking.

There are many agents who deal with television scriptwriters and the advice contained in Chapter 15, 'Agents and publishers', will help you with those. Also look for the names of producers on the end credits of programmes you admire. If you think that your work is in a similar area, then these will be names to send your spec script to ('spec' is simply short for speculative and means a script that no one has commissioned). It should, by now, go without saying that you should read plenty of examples of scripts before writing your own. And, of course, watch as many quality examples of your chosen formats as you can. Become an expert in your chosen medium.

WHERE TO SEND YOUR CALLING CARD SCRIPT

The Writers' and Artists' Yearbook contains a comprehensive list of all the main production companies, together with information about the kind of projects they are involved in. Another route into television is the BBC Writers' Room – www.bbc.co.uk/writersroom.

Writing collaboratively

More than any other medium, television writing is one where collaboration is common. Indeed, it is the norm in some genres. Many new shows have a lead writer, known as a 'show-runner', who leads a committee writing process where ideas are batted about and lines are argued over until it is quite unclear who is the final writer on any one episode. This has been common practice in American television writing for years but is quite new to the UK, which has for a long time held out for the primacy of the single writer.

Many writers enjoy the challenge of working collaboratively, though it demands flexibility and tolerance from those involved in it. If you work in television or film, you will be working collaboratively with producers, directors, actors, commissioning executives, story editors and script editors in any case. It is therefore a relatively straightforward step to working with another writer.

More good ideas

If it is working well, a collaboration more than doubles the qualities that each writer brings to the mix. Your good idea provokes another good idea from your partner, which provokes a better idea from you and so on. The competitive energy of this kind of piggyback thinking means that you can move forward with a story faster than either of you could on your own. Your partner might spot weak lines and implausible events before you can, while you might have a much better idea for how to resolve Act III than they do.

I would never attempt to write a novel or a story with another writer, but there is something about the story-driven and visual impulse of television that makes it right for collaborative work. Of course, you need to be able to fight for your ideas and sometimes the partnership won't feel like an equal one. If it was your initial idea the final result might be 70:30 yours; there may even be times when whole segments or whole episodes are 90:10. What you hope is that the work will balance out over time.

THE SONGWRITING MODEL

The best model for collaborative working is probably the songwriting partnership of John Lennon and Paul McCartney of The Beatles. The two of them wrote fairly few 50:50 compositions, but instead brought unfinished work to one another for completion. Sometimes they would bring complete, finished numbers to each other for checking and quality control. These would then be worked up and arranged in the studio with the rest of the band and their producer.

Television is very different from songwriting but the impulse behind a good collaboration should be the same. You should achieve more together than either of you would do separately. Writing together, you should add up to more than the sum of your parts. For example, one partner might have a measured, thoughtful way of working that complements the more spontaneous approach of the other and also often act as a brake on the wilder instincts. Writing for television on one's own is perfectly possible, but working with a partner is often more enjoyable.

Writing in tandem with someone else is not for everyone – it can be frustrating to have to justify your ideas, though in television you will always have to do that sooner or later, so it's best perhaps to do it at an early stage with a friend rather than with a coldly professional commissioning executive. It's definitely worth experimenting with.

 ## Teamworking

A lot of television is written by teams (this is especially true in the United States). Programmes have a 'show-runner', a lead writer responsible for the shape of the programme who will work with a team who will all chip in ideas and stories, even for those episodes that others will write.

Write with a partner

Meet for one afternoon with another writer whose work you admire. They can be from a writers' group or someone you know socially with an interest in writing. Each of you must bring three ideas for stories to the meeting. Agree in advance that this collaboration is a one-off. Decide which of the ideas is best and try to work up a one-page outline. You'll know from this short experiment whether further collaboration is for you, or whether you are a lone wolf.

Writing for film

Television treats writers rather better than the film industry does. With film, the first question to be asked of any project is 'Who's the star?' – whereas with television they do at least ask 'Who are the writers?'

The most obvious difference between film and television is that television shrinks stories to less than life size and so perhaps makes more noise and melodrama to compensate. Film, on the other hand, blows up characters and stories to many times human scale. This means, paradoxically, that good film writing is about restraint and understatement.

Ingmar Bergman

'The theatre is like a faithful wife. The film is the great adventure – the costly exacting mistress.'

TV vs. film

Television is essentially a domestic, often solitary experience, while film is a communal event.

Films are never serials. They follow a three-act structure during which time we must get to know all the characters well and have an emotional investment in them.

There is, in the UK at least, almost no demand for British film writers. Very few full-length British films are made and those that are often don't make it into cinemas. And those that get as far as the multiplexes are usually written by a handful of highly experienced writers with great track records, such as Peter Morgan (*The Queen*), Tim Firth (*Calendar Girls*) and Richard Curtis (*Four Weddings and a Funeral*), all of whom wrote extensively for television first.

Star talent

The film producer Nik Powell (*Scandal*, *The Crying Game*, etc.) once gave a lecture where he said that his idea of a good script was 'one that the talent likes'. If you can get big-name talent attached, you are a lot further forward with your project, whether it is for film or television. There's no mystery to how this is done. If you have a film script you are proud of, you can send it to the agent of your star and hope that they love it enough to consider the role. This in turn gives you some leverage with the various power brokers that put together film financing. It helps if it is your agent punting the script towards the star's agent, if only because it means that you have some track record within the industry, some clout.

The problem is, of course, that the 'talent' has no more informed an idea of what constitutes a good script than anyone else. Indeed, their judgement might be clouded by all sorts of random factors such as 'How long am I on screen for?', 'Will the script make me look ridiculous?', 'Who is my love interest?'. These questions might be very important to the star but getting the answers they want doesn't mean that the script is a good one.

You may not ever get the star you dream of when writing a film, but it is worth at least having an actor in mind when writing it. This can provide you with an important focus. If you can't think of an actor that might fit the film, then perhaps your characters aren't as clearly defined as you had thought. Or perhaps your film is out of step with the current marketplace. This is not necessarily a bad thing, but it does mean that perhaps you should look at your characters again.

Cast your characters

Choose a story you have written and cast it in your head. Now read the story again. Does your idea of the characters change when you imagine them as specific actors?

Those who rail against the star system should consider just how much it costs to make a mainstream feature film. Even for a relatively low-budget British film, you can be talking upwards of £20 million. With this kind of money at stake it is no wonder that producers will do all they can to protect their investment and, like it or not, who the lead actors are is top of most people's list when it comes to deciding what movie to see.

The short film

There is a way to become a film writer without having a track record already, and that is to write a short film. Many organizations are dedicated to providing writing and directing opportunities for those interested in short films. Audiences are tiny and opportunities to exhibit the films are generally limited to specialist festivals, but nevertheless it is something that the novice film writer should consider.

Most short films are between 5 and 15 minutes long and in that time they must do everything that a feature-length piece would do. We must care about the characters, those characters must face some kind of threat, be in some kind of jeopardy, and we must feel that we, like them, have been on some kind of mental journey by the time we emerge blinking into reality. It's difficult to pull off in 90 minutes and harder still in ten. But if you can produce an interesting ten-minute script, producers are more likely to want to see longer work.

The Internet has made it much easier than ever before to find an outlet for your work. A good film put out on the Internet has a chance of gaining a respectable audience as word spreads virally across the web.

Workshop exercise

By now you should have a lot of ideas with the potential to become scripts for a short film. Choose one. It could be the script you started working on in Chapter 12 on stage plays and continued to develop in Chapter 13 on writing radio plays. It could be a short story you'd like to turn into a script. It could be something completely new. Whatever your idea, these questions should help you think about developing it for the screen.

1. Who would be on your dream cast list for your short film? Try to aim for at least three, but no more than six, main characters.

2. Does your story stick to the three-act structure? Make sure you have a strong beginning, middle and end.

3. Is there anyone with whom you could collaborate on your script? Perhaps the writer you met with in the collaboration exercise above? Ask them for ideas or input that could improve your film script.

4. Is your timing right? Read your script out loud and time it.

5. Look online and find five places to submit your script.

Jenny Lecoat

'*Television is essentially collaborative. No matter how many months you have spent working alone on your script, and no matter how many times you may have rewritten and redrafted it before submission, remember that, for the person reading it, it is still a first draft. And, even if that person loves it, there will be many more drafts.*'

(*Jenny Lecoat has written for many of the top soap operas in the UK and the United States and has also worked as a stand-up comedian.*)

Where to next?

That's it for our discussions of different forms of creative writing. We've covered everything from short stories to film scripts and hopefully you've tried your hand at a few. In the next chapter we'll be looking at what comes next – finding a home for your work with an agent or publisher.

15

Agents and publishers

As a new writer you have one huge advantage over
the competition: you are a fresh voice. You are offering
something different. If you are on your fourth novel and the
last three sold, say, 5,000 each, your publisher could be
forgiven for thinking that this one too will sell 5,000 copies.
Why should you suddenly sell millions now? Whereas a new
voice might just catch hold of the public imagination and
make mega-bucks for all concerned. The publishing industry
needs new writers or there's no industry at all.

How do you go about getting published? This chapter
aims to give you the inside track on the role of agents and
publishers and advice on how to go about finding the right
agent to represent you. You'll also learn about publishing
outside the mainstream. There are also some useful tips on
how to cope with rejection.

How not to get published

What happens when you've written your book? Well, you check it carefully for typos, pick a publisher from the *Writers' and Artists' Yearbook* and send it off, together with a polite covering letter that more or less approximates to the lyrics of The Beatles' 'Paperback Writer'.

After a few weeks a letter comes back offering you a deal and a huge advance.

A couple of months after that a cheque arrives and with it the beautiful cover. The proofs arrive and you correct them (not that there's much to correct) and some weeks after that the (glowing) reviews are appearing; the book is on the shelves of every high-street bookshop in the land; the Chinese translation rights have been sold; Steven Spielberg is making a movie with Johnny Depp in the lead role; and you are swigging back fine wines in discreet city clubs with the cream of the literati. Zadie Smith has got your mobile number and uses it. You're a regular on *Question Time* and *Oprah*; you've just been asked to appear on *Desert Island Discs*; and Ivy League universities are bidding for your manuscripts and letters and shopping lists.

You wish.

The reality is that if you simply send your manuscript off to a publisher you will be placed on the slush pile. This is a filing cabinet full of manuscripts awaiting the attention of a 17-year-old intern who might, if you are lucky, pass your book on upwards if they feel that it has any merit. The intern might be a gifted and perceptive reader, but they're also going to be very busy answering the phone, ordering paper for the photocopier and making coffee for the more senior executives. They're also very quickly going to suffer from novel fatigue as they try to stay enthusiastic about yet another Second World War romance.

Avoiding the slush pile

Just sticking your manuscript, however brilliant, into an envelope and punting it off to publishers is not giving it your best shot. It is the equivalent of turning up on a date late, scruffy, unwashed and skint. It shows a lack of respect towards the industry and towards your own work. In the first instance, what you need to do is find an agent.

Why do you need an agent?

Having a good agent is like having a native guide through hostile territory. A good agent is not a counsellor, a social worker, a teacher, an editor, a lawyer, an expert in industrial relations or a psychotherapist, though at times they might seem like all these things. They are not really your mate either, not at first, though with luck they may become one. A good agent is your champion in the publishing world. For 10 or 15 per cent of your earnings, they will try to find the most suitable editor at the publisher best placed to promote your work well.

Having found a publisher, they will negotiate fees, often including fees for audio books, film rights and foreign sales. And before all this they will also often do the work that editors used to do but don't really any more. A skilful agent reads your work for its literary merit, but also with their knowledge of the current marketplace. They will make suggestions for ways to improve your manuscript, which are usually worth following. Bear in mind that they like your writing – that's why they took you on in the first place – so what they have to say about your book is made with your best interests as a writer at heart.

The trouble is that – like many really good things – they can be hard to find.

Fred Allen

'My agent gets ten per cent of everything I get, except my blinding headaches.'

Aspiring writers often have negative things to say about agents, just as they do about publishing in general. This is probably to do with the arbitrary power they seem to wield. An agent's thumbs down can seem as damning to the new writer as any given by the old Roman emperors in the Colosseum. But generally agents love books. They spend all their time reading books or talking about books or thinking about books. Would they do that if they were really just cynical salespeople? There must be easier ways of making a good living than wading through the literary outpourings of the public. So what if agents want to make money? That's fair enough, isn't it? After all, so do you.

On the money

In my experience, if you eavesdrop on a conversation between professional writers they are likely to be talking about money, while two agents are quite likely to be talking about literature.

Having an agent is doubly useful because publishers use them as a filter. If you have succeeded in convincing an agent that there is potential in your book, then publishers are much more likely to take notice.

Focus point

Many publishers – particularly the bigger ones – will only look at work submitted to them via an agent. Agents build up a relationship with editors, so that when editors receive a submission they know that someone they trust thinks it is a book they will like and that will sell.

How to get an agent

Writers often go about trying to find agents in the wrong way. They just mail a manuscript to an agency and then hope for the best. Do this and you are probably wasting a stamp.

You want an agent who is going to be sympathetic to your work, so it is worth doing some research. First-time novelists will always thank their agents somewhere on the book, so if you have read a first novel you have enjoyed and whose work seems to be in a similar area to yours, then that agent might be a possibility. Use the Internet to find out which established writers agents represent. Agents often give talks at literary festivals, so go along and hear what they have to say.

WHEN TO CONTACT AN AGENT

It is best to wait until you have finished your book and got it into its best possible shape. This means at least a second, possibly even a third, full draft. If an agent accepts you on the strength of 60 brilliant pages, and the rest of the book is theoretical at this stage, misunderstandings can occur. The book you eventually produce might well be some distance from the book the agent thought you were producing. Cue disappointment all round.

Focus point

Many – most – agents will have numerous clients that they are already looking after and they may just be too busy to give you the attention your work needs. They may not be simply giving you the brush-off when they say that their lists are full. With this in mind, you should try finding newer agents who are still building a list. You could try phoning the receptionist and finding out who has recently joined the firm.

MAKING YOUR APPROACH

When you have a list of potential agents, this is how to approach them:

- Send them the first 60 pages of your book, together with a polite, short covering letter.

  Don't send them the whole manuscript. If they like the opening pages, then they'll ask for the rest. Send your pages in a proper padded envelope/mailer. Don't use one of those made from recycled cardboard that will explode in a cloud of grey chaff when your would-be agent tears it open. If you have just ruined their favourite outfit, the agent is unlikely to look upon your work as favourably as they might have done otherwise.

- Don't send a synopsis.

  This is controversial advice, we know, and many other people will say you should always send one. What's the point? If they don't like the first 60 pages, they are unlikely to say to themselves, 'But look how it ends!' If they like the first 60 pages, they'll eventually read the whole book anyway.

- Send your work to several agents simultaneously.

  Again, this is controversial advice but it means that if one agent rings you up asking to meet, then you can call the others, saying that you are having a meeting with Agent X and could you perhaps meet them too? At the very least this will ensure that they read your work pretty quickly.

Focus point

Contrary to popular opinion, agents will always read your work. Of course they will. Every single agent has their own personal nightmare where they turned down J. K. Rowling. Every single one fears going down in history as the next Dick Rowe. (Dick Rowe was the man who turned down The Beatles when he was at Decca Records.) All work gets read properly eventually, so be patient.

Not their job

Don't use agents as the first sounding boards for your work. This is not their job.

THE COVERING LETTER

This should be short and polite and employ judicious flattery: 'I've heard that you are a fantastic agent and you represent X whose work I very much admire ...' Don't write too much about yourself, just that which is interesting. Don't mention your job unless it's a very interesting one or relevant to the book. You are selling yourself as well as the work. Do mention any courses you've taken such as those with the Arvon Foundation. Mention, too, any successes you have had with writing, prizes won or stories published. If you have a track record, let them know. Don't forget to include your contact details.

Send your letter to a named agent. Simply sending it to the agency will mean that it could end up anywhere, including on the desk of the newest intern. You can follow up with a phone call but wait at least a few weeks before you do this.

Write a practice letter

The covering letter is the last thing you will write before you send off your work, but it is the first thing that an agent or a publisher will read, so practise writing a good covering letter. Before you send it make sure you get it proofread by a competent, literate friend.

222

MEETING AGENTS

If you get the chance, shop around for agents. You might be lucky and find that the first agent you approach agrees to take you on. However, it is important to make sure that you can work together happily. No doubt many agents will be razor-sharp, hardworking, thoughtful and passionate about books, but what about their other qualities? You may want someone personable, someone with whom you can have a laugh, or you may prefer someone known to be 'a Rottweiler', a notorious terrorizer of publishers who generally plays hardball in every aspect of life.

Not all agents are good. Anyone can set themselves up as an agent, which is another reason for doing your research first. Know who else they represent and meet them in their offices to decide whether you can trust them.

An agent's dealings with the business end of things need to be professional. Their comments on your work also need to be astute, but this is not to say that you should always take their advice. However, they are the experts and, if you decide to trust your judgement rather than theirs, be prepared to be wrong. A good agent may not press the point but will often be proved right.

Publishers

If you keep writing for any length of time, you will begin to hear a lot of moaning about publishers. Some of it is justified. However, one thing that should keep you from falling prey to a debilitating despair is the fact that writers have always been complaining about the publishing industry.

It is true that publishers face some difficult times. Reading as a leisure pursuit is in decline, squeezed by the plethora of noisier alternatives. The big bookselling chains and the supermarkets demand huge discounts, which eat into publishers' already small profit margin.

Books have a much shorter shelf-life than they once did. If the book doesn't shift copies in the first few weeks, then it is off the shelves and heading back to the warehouse. The carefully crafted books that take a year of agony to write are less in demand than ever before. Instead, the ghosted celebrity memoir, fitness bibles, cookbooks and television tie-ins dominate.

Publishers, you will hear it said, are no longer the family-run outfits of a presumed Golden Age (which always seems to be the 1950s, just after the war and just before rock and roll), but instead are mostly part of huge multinationals that care more about profits for the shareholders than about literature or writing.

SMALL COGS IN A BIG MACHINE

Authors are so many cogs in a machine producing units for mass consumption, and if the masses don't want a serious volume of the units you produce, then let's get somebody else in. Let's try to turn another – preferably young and good-looking – writer into a brand. Better still, let's find an established young and good-looking brand – a pop star or a footballer's girlfriend – and see if we can squeeze some units out of that.

The independent bookshops are all closing, Amazon is selling books with huge discounts, Tesco and Walmart sell them for still less and even libraries have become Internet cafés where the loaning out of books is just a sideline to their real business of helping the long-term unemployed brush up their computer skills. All this and worse is what you'll hear and there's some truth to it.

It seems that in the old days writers were allowed to grow and develop, to build a following. Publishers would keep faith with an author over several books, not necessarily making money until quite late on in a writer's career. Not now. These days, instant returns are demanded. And even if those instant returns are achieved, then they must be equalled with the next book. Even well-established authors live in fear of their books being rejected.

Focus point

Surprising – and heartwarming – fact: according to an article in a recent *London Review of Books*, the book trade in the UK is worth rather more than the bread industry – around £9 billion, in fact. And the US book industry is still worth $80 billion. And you have the advantage of writing in English. Foreign publishers buy far more books of ours than we do of theirs. Last year, for example, only around 40 of the 100,000 books published in German were translated into English. Even the winner of the German equivalent of the Man Booker prize wasn't published in English.

Despite this, publishing houses, like literary agencies, are staffed by people who love books. They really love books, to the point of being obsessed by them. In fact, more books are published in the UK than ever before. The industry still makes money.

FRESH TALENT

Publishers still want to find the next big thing. And yes, of course they are tempted to invest in the young and good-looking, but there are plenty of inspiring stories about older first-time writers. Marina Lewycka (*A Short History of Tractors in Ukrainian*), Alice Sebold (*The Lovely Bones*) and Mary Wesley (*The Camomile Lawn*) had all been writing unsuccessfully for years before they were picked up and became household names.

There are still some very big advances being offered to writers. You'll have no doubt read about those in six figures, but these headline figures don't generally stand up to too much scrutiny. Say a writer gets £100,000 ($150,000). This might well be for three books with just one-third paid upon signing. The rest of the money is paid as further books are delivered.

If each book takes, on average, two years from first idea to first print run, then that is actually slightly less than £17,000 ($25,000) per year, a figure that actually compares rather badly with being a nurse or a teacher. And that's for a huge advance; most are much smaller. The average advance for a first novel is about £3,000 ($4,500). J. K. Rowling's first advance was £1,500 ($2,250) paid in two instalments. And if a writer gets a huge advance, then they need huge sales. Should those sales not be forthcoming, then they are likely to be dumped with very little ceremony. And who wants to be an ex-novelist?

Some people make a lot of money from books. But I guess it won't be us, not yet anyway. Generally, the more a publisher pays for a book, the more they will invest in promoting a book. Authors don't want the big advances just because they're greedy but because they want a publisher to get behind their book with advertising and promotion. Publishers that have invested a lot of hard cash will energize their sales teams; will organize special events; will make sure your books are visible in the shops. (They do this by paying for display space. While independent bookshops will put whoever they want in the window or in prominent piles in the shop, the big chains have sold this display space to publishers.)

Small presses

It is true that there are fewer mainstream publishers than ever before (many of the imprints turn out to be owned by the same company), but changes in the printing and distribution industry have meant that there are numerous small presses, many with very good reputations, which succeed in developing the careers of their writers. Some of these writers are happy to stay with the publishers who discovered them; others move up to the bigger league.

Nurturing talent

You could argue that the genuine nurseries for new writing talent are the small independent publishers.

Many independent publishers are kitchen-table affairs – they are book enthusiasts trying to publish half a dozen titles on a shoestring. These are people who only publish books they genuinely like instead of trying to second-guess the marketplace. Because of this, they often score some real surprise successes. Before submitting your book to the small presses, however, do them the courtesy of treating them professionally. Make sure that you get hold of some of their other titles. Read them. Follow the publisher's submission guidelines carefully.

If you go with a small press, it may be unlikely that you'll be able to stroll into your local Waterstones or Barnes & Noble and see the book on the shelf. But direct sales from publishers are becoming more important, even for the big companies. And the one big advantage of the rise of Amazon is that there now exists a warehouse where readers can get hold of virtually every book that there has ever been. Books stay on the shelves of bookshops for a shorter time than ever before but, paradoxically, they remain available for ever.

Digital self-publishing

There exist a number of companies who will agree, for a fee, to publish your book. This is known as vanity publishing and something to be avoided unless you are a) very wealthy and b) very self-confident.

You can, of course, become a publisher yourself and control the whole process from editing and cover design to marketing and distribution. You can do this the old-fashioned way, by ordering multiple copies of your book from a printer, but with advances in print-on-demand technology from sites like Lulu, the process is now much more affordable and convenient.

These days, though, a book doesn't have to be printed to be read. There are many websites that will allow you to create and distribute an ebook that can be read on an e-reader, a tablet, a laptop or even a mobile phone. This means no agents, no publishers and a much, much bigger share of the profits. Tempting, especially when you hear about success stories like Huw Howey, whose ebook trilogy *Wool* was not only picked up by a publisher but is also being made into a film by Ridley Scott. Conversely – not that you need reminding – for every breakthrough star there are countless other writers whose only loyal reader is their mum.

If you are considering self-publishing, whether digitally or by having your books printed, there are some things you need to take into account. You are taking on the mantle of editor, proofreader, designer and promoter and these are all specialist tasks that can take years to master. Even if you can pay someone to do them for you, getting the books into the shops, getting press reviews and getting actual sales is much harder.

People in the self-publishing world often cite the 80/20 rule, which means that, to be a successful self-publisher – or self-e-publisher – you need to spend 80 per cent of your time editing, formatting, designing, marketing and promoting your work, and the remaining 20 per cent actually writing it. Successful self-publishing requires a large amount of social networking, so if you're averse to living on Twitter and Facebook and in online forums then this is probably not for you.

For many writers this will be like a bucket of cold water. The idea of sacrificing so much precious writing time will be untenable. The idea of doing all the 'boring' bits – the proofreading, the formatting – will be equally repellent.

Also, part of the desire to be published springs from the need for validation. We need to know whether what we have to say is worth hearing. And how can we know that if we have become our own publisher? It is important for your self-esteem as a writer to know that others have invested their precious time, talent and energy into your work.

If all of this puts you off the idea of self-publishing, that's fine. But if the thought of going it alone excites you, if you love social networking, if you're a confident self-promoter, if you have an eye for design, if you're a genius salesperson or if you just don't need much sleep, then dive in and have a go. Many people see digital self-publishing as liberating, a way of returning control to the author. Of course, when you self-publish a book, you also get to keep all the profit – if there is any.

Perhaps, though, we're getting a bit ahead of ourselves. Self-publishing a complete work is something you should consider when your manuscript is not only finished but polished to a high gleam, but that's not to say there aren't many ways self-publishing can be a great tool for the developing writer.

Focus point

Self-publishing is simpler and cheaper than ever, and for some writers it has led to huge success. However, it is a complicated and risky process that takes a great deal of time and effort, and you shouldn't undertake it until your work is completely finished.

Workshop exercise

Here are some questions that should help you decide whether or not your work is ready to be published online.

1. Have you edited and redrafted your work to the best of your abilities, following the advice given in this book? Has your work done its time in the drawer?
2. Have you given your book to several trusted readers and then applied their advice to your next draft?
3. Has your book been checked and checked and checked again for spelling mistakes and grammatical errors?
4. Have you thoroughly researched your potential markets and platforms?
5. Do you know how to format your work properly?
6. Do you have a marketing plan?

If you answered 'no' to any of these questions, then stop. You're not ready yet.

Internet publishing for fun, not profit

For those at the beginning of their writing journey the Internet, if handled correctly, can function as the biggest writing workshop in the world. Writers can be shy creatures, not overly fond of venturing from their garrets, and the Internet offers an opportunity to find a community of other writers and readers without having to change out of your pyjamas.

Some websites like Wattpad and Figment allow you to post stories or individual chapters of your book so that other users of the site can comment, make suggestions and offer feedback and encouragement. Sites like Authonomy let you upload an entire book. To make the most of sites like this, you need to give as much as you take – make sure you read other people's work and try to leave thoughtful, constructive comments. It's just good manners and you'll find that you quickly make friends, possibly even fans. You might even be one of the success stories yourself, like Abbie Gibbs, the teenage author whose Wattpad-published book *The Dark Heroine* was picked up by HarperCollins for a six-figure advance.

Go online

Go online and have a look at a site like Wattpad, Authonomy or Figment. Pick the genre that you would like to write in, or one you like to read, and have a look at the work. What do you think? Read some of the feedback other users have left – would you find this useful?

Sites like this can be a great place to try out some of your wilder ideas, too. Genre fiction is hugely popular online, so if you like writing SF, fantasy, horror or even erotica, you might find your people on the web. There are sites devoted to 'fan fiction', where writers take characters from their favourite books, films, television programmes or games and write new stories about them. It's great fun and the writing can be excellent, not to mention hilarious. Beware, though – there is often an 'adult' side to these communities so, if you don't want to ruin your image of Harry Potter, be careful where you click.

Focus point

Publishing online doesn't have to be about making a profit. It can be a way to develop and strengthen your work, find a community of like-minded writers or just have some fun.

Zines

If you want to go right back to basics, though, and if you're one of those people who looks back wistfully on arts and crafts sessions at school, then you might enjoy making a zine, probably the most low-tech form of publishing there is. Zines (short for magazines) are small, handmade booklets, often embellished with collages or drawings. They grew out of the punk scene in the '70s, when people would create 'fanzines' about their favourite bands and distribute them at gigs. Over the years the form has developed and now zines are swapped or sold online through 'distros' or at zine fairs – these take place all over the UK and the United States and a quick Internet search will tell you where the nearest one is.

You can make a zine about absolutely anything you want. The point of a zine is that it is an unfettered expression of you and your creativity, swapped with a community of like-minded people. A zine is pure creative fun, and that's the important thing to remember about writing, especially when you're just starting out. Being published doesn't have to be the end game. You don't have to bother about any of that if you don't feel like it. Writing can be (whisper it) just something you do for yourself, because you love it and because you can.

Make a zine

1. Get four sheets of printer paper. Fold them in half to make a booklet and staple or sew them in the middle. You now have 18 pages to play with.

2. Choose a theme. It can be literally anything you want. If you're stuck, use one of the journal prompts from Chapter 2.

3. Plan roughly what you want to include on each page.

4. Go crazy. Write, draw, glue in pictures cut from magazines or printed from the Internet. Experiment. As we discussed in Chapter 2, sometimes dabbling in a new form of creativity can be rejuvenating, and making a mess is always fun.

Coping with rejection

Who knew that the rejections you need are those of the most crushing kind? Nice ones are just too upsetting.

When your agent starts sending out your first book, he or she will probably choose several editors. They might all reject you, but their responses could vary from the brutally dismissive to the lukewarm to the heartbreakingly enthusiastic. Being turned down by someone who says that they 'absolutely loved' the book is far harder to deal with than the ones who give a curt 'this is not for me'. It's because it seems to leave you with nowhere to go. If even the editors that love the book won't put it out, what do you do then?

You write another book, that's what.

If you're at an earlier stage than this and getting rejections from agents or publishers that keep mentioning the same things (lack of pace, too much backstory, etc.) then perhaps you need to rework your manuscript once more, addressing these concerns.

You can always console yourself with the thought that J. K. Rowling's book *Harry Potter and the Philosopher's Stone* was turned down by nine publishers and Stephen King was rejected 84 times before publishing his first short story. Robert Pirsig was turned down by a staggering 122 publishers before going on to sell millions of his classic *Zen and the Art of Motorcycle Maintenance*. Even Zadie Smith was rejected by HarperCollins before all her successes with Penguin.

Focus point

Rejections are a badge of honour, battle scars in the fight to produce your very best work. The desire to prove the critics wrong should spur you on all the more.

Camilla Hornby

'*Agents and publishers are people too, just busy people, so make your approach concise and literate and make the material as good as it can be before sending it in.*'

(*Camilla Hornby is an agent at Curtis Brown.*)

Where to next?

We're nearly at the end of our journey. By now you should have a whole host of ideas and with any luck some finished pieces you're proud of. Some of you will want to take your learning further, and the next chapter looks at ways to do that and organizations that can help.

16

Moving on

If you have enjoyed the exercises in this book, you will be feeling more confident in your writing than you were a few weeks or months ago. You may now feel ready to join the wider writing community – if you haven't already. Feeling yourself to be a part of that wider world can make the business of writing – the business of perseverance – seem less painful. Yes, writing is something you do largely on your own, but there is a family of writers, too.

There are many creative writing classes, courses and writers' circles that you could join and you may also want to gain a formal qualification such as a degree or diploma. This chapter also tells you where to find creative writing courses and about literary festivals.

Creative writing classes

Perhaps you have some short stories that feel finished and that you are happy with. Perhaps you have sent some off to competitions. Maybe you have a novel developing, or a play or a screenplay. You will definitely have a notebook bulging with ideas.

If you have managed some of this on your own, then you have proved that you have the true writer's ability to deal with solitude. You have self-discipline and perseverance and these are the two most important qualities you need as a writer. However, creative writing classes can help you develop your skills more quickly, as you also learn from your fellow classmates' successes and failures.

Nathaniel Hawthorne

'The only sensible ends of literature are, first, the pleasurable toil of writing; second, the gratification of one's family and friends; and, lastly the solid cash.'

There was a time when local authorities ran evening classes in almost everything and creative writing would definitely be on the curriculum somewhere. These classes seem very much geared to the world of work these days, and so finding those which develop the spirit, or what Ted Hughes called 'the imagination of the tribe', seems harder than it was. Nevertheless, some enlightened councils still offer creative writing classes and it's worth contacting the arts or culture department of your council to find out whether they are running them. The public library should also have details of courses in your area.

The Workers Educational Association (WEA) also runs classes of all kinds, and very often creative writing is part of their programme. The WEA courses are also very inexpensive.

Calvin Coolidge

'Nothing in this world can take the place of persistence. Talent will not; nothing is more common than unsuccessful people with talent. Genius will not; unrewarded genius is almost a proverb. Education will not; the world is full of educated

The Arvon Foundation

We've referred to Arvon several times in the course of this book. This is because the Arvon formula really works. Set up by poets John Moat and John Fairfax in 1968, an Arvon course (run from various rural locations in the UK) sees up to 16 students working with two professional writers for five days. The alchemy of workshops, discussions, readings, one-to-one feedback, being surrounded by other writers and no distractions, really does push students to make giant strides with their writing. A third professional writer comes as the midweek guest reader to provide yet another positive element to the mix.

The list of tutors who have worked for Arvon is hugely impressive. Novelists such as Stan Barstow, Suzanne Berne, Mavis Cheek, Jill Dawson, Suzannah Dunn, Kathryn Heyman, Hanif Kureishi, Deborah Levy, Toby Litt, Thomas Lynch, Caryl Phillips, Will Self, Sarah Waters and Edmund White have all worked with Arvon recently. All the leading contemporary poets including Simon Armitage, Carol Ann Duffy, Daljit Nagra, Hugo Williams, and many others, have worked at Arvon. Other guests have been playwrights such as Willy Russell and Simon Stephens; television writers like Jimmy McGovern; and film directors like Anthony Minghella.

I'm sure the secret of Arvon's success is the sense of purposeful, creative endeavour and good fellowship that a week spent writing without worrying about work, children, spouses or any of the daily grind engenders. And 'no distractions' really does mean just that. There is no Internet, no email, no television, no radio; just good company in a beautiful setting.

Arvon has created brilliant writers, too: Booker prize-winner Pat Barker started writing on an Arvon course, as did the prize-winning novelist Lesley Glaister, as well as well-known poets like Neil Rollinson, Carole Satyamurti and Michael Laskey.

You will find that friendships formed with your fellow students provide you with constructive candid readers, and supportive relationships that will sustain you through years of writing.

Similar operations to Arvon are run at Ty Newydd in Wales, and Moniack Mhor in Scotland, which provide a range of exciting courses for writers at all levels. These include courses for those who want to write in Welsh or in Gaelic. Both houses are historic and in beautiful locations. Moniack Mhor is in the most evocative part of the Highlands, close to Loch Ness, while Ty Newydd is on the Welsh coast at Cricieth and is the former home of David Lloyd George.

You can find out about Arvon's courses at www.arvonfoundation.org.

Literary festivals and conferences

Literary festivals are great places to see and hear your favourite writers, and to find out about the great writers of the future. As well as talks and readings by writers, many literary festivals run workshops and master-classes in which you can participate.

Conferences, too, are places where writers gather and, in addition to the useful lectures and workshops, many important writing friendships can be formed at mealtimes and in the bar.

Writers' circles

You might want to join a writers' circle (they can have other names). The idea behind a writers' circle is that you read one another's work (presumably sitting in a circle) in turn. It gives you a chance to have your work read, or heard, by other writers who will provide valuable feedback.

When looking for a writers' circle there are several things to consider.

FREQUENCY OF MEETINGS

If you are looking for feedback, you want a group that meets regularly and frequently and one that goes on meeting through the summer holidays.

VENUE

Private houses are not the best venues for writers' circles, as they encourage chat rather than serious discussion of writing. Ideally, your group should meet on neutral ground such as in a school or a library. Otherwise it is too much of a social occasion.

FEEDBACK

Different groups have different rules about feedback. In an ideal world, every writers' circle would give plenty of time for discussion of manuscripts and that discussion would be frank but never discouraging. You will need a good chairperson who will ensure that everyone gets the airtime they need and that the meetings aren't dominated by the same garrulous voices every week.

I think these kinds of groups work best when they consider just one or two chunks of manuscript at a session. These extracts should have been circulated in advance so that those commenting on them can read them properly rather than being expected to respond on a first hearing or a cursory read. People whose works are being discussed should not be allowed to contribute to the discussion until the end, when everyone else has had their say.

This may seem unduly harsh, but it means that the writer is forced to listen to the whole debate about their work without getting defensive or trying to explain complicated plot points. It allows those giving the feedback to talk freely, knowing that the author isn't going to jump down their throat.

Each circle will have its own way of doing things, but a good one will let you sit in for a few evenings to see whether it is for you. Most of these groups charge a small subscription for membership.

The creative writing MA

Not so long ago there were only a couple of these in the UK. In the United States they are much more established. Most people know of the one at University of East Anglia set up by Malcolm Bradbury (though it wasn't the first; that honour goes to Lancaster University), but there are now more than a hundred in the UK.

Most universities now offer a creative writing MA to those with a first degree in any discipline. All of the universities will have some kind of entrance criteria. This may be a request to look at your work, or an interview, or both. Most universities offer both full-time and part-time courses. In 2010 the fees for this MA were around £3,500.

These are most useful for the concentrated time they allow you to write, and for the support and solidarity you will get from other students. The support you get from the tutors varies, of course. Many great writers are not necessarily great teachers. Others may not do all that much teaching anyway, their presence in a university being mainly symbolic. Often the universities who have the best creative departments are not those with the most famous writers as their tutors, but those staffed by working writers with a genuine commitment to helping their students to progress.

With many of these courses there is no longer the expectation that all the students will move seamlessly from completing their MA to publication. Most students who successfully obtain degrees will not become published authors, and it is as well to know this before you begin.

THE DISTANCE-LEARNING MA

Following an online course gives you the chance to study from home. There will usually be a programme of reading as well as academic work marked by the lecturers. You may well also have an opportunity to 'meet' your fellow students in a university-hosted chat room once a week to critique each other's work. These sessions are often hosted by professional tutors.

This process will be helpful to your own writing because the other students are likely to be both fair and candid in their appraisal of your work, expecting the same from you in return. It will also be interesting because you will get the chance to talk regularly with literature enthusiasts from all over the world. Distance-learning students can be based anywhere, not just in the country where the course is based.

Online study has its disadvantages (lack of personal contact; doesn't get you away from the computer screen), but you may find the mixture of students' backgrounds, interests and ages exhilarating. You might find many fine writers among your students and want to keep in touch with them afterwards, whether or not you go on to be published.

Undergraduate degrees and diplomas

Universities and colleges are now beginning to offer courses for those who do not already have a degree and perhaps this will be more suitable for you. Degree courses are generally three years (full time) and several have creative writing as a component with other arts subjects, such as English or Film Studies. Diploma courses tend to be shorter.

Literary consultancies

A number of organizations will offer professional critiques of your work for a fee. Quite a few writers now top up their incomes by offering this service, while others work for established consultancies. The best known is also the oldest: the Literary Consultancy (see 'Taking it further') was founded in 1996 and has a very good reputation for using highly qualified writers to offer comprehensive candid feedback within a reasonably short timeframe. Others may not be so reputable. It is always worth finding other writers who have used the services of a particular consultancy before committing any money. At the time of writing, fees for recognized consultancies work out at about £1 for a page of critiqued work, or £300 ($450) or so to get rigorous feedback on a complete novel.

The award-winning writer Jill Dawson helps organize Gold Dust, which offers mentoring as well as feedback on writing. Several other quite well-known writers also offer similar services privately.

There are numerous other very reputable literary consultancies and you can find their addresses in the *Writers' and Artists' Yearbook*.

Mentoring

Hanif Kureishi once said that it was impossible for any writer to break through on their own. Everyone, however gifted, needs guidance through the process. Mentoring of this sort has become commonplace and, if you are serious about developing your writing, you will be encouraged to become involved in this process.

Gold Dust is one writer-led mentoring programme that provides a number of one-to-one sessions with highly respected professionals, in addition to a personalized feedback service. There are other

239

private initiatives of this sort, as well as charitable ones such as those organized by the Jerwood Foundation, and several schemes organized by Arts Council England. The Arts Council will occasionally support new writers who wish to purchase the services of established writers to work with them and it is always worth building a relationship with your regional Literature Officer. (See 'Taking it further' for more information on these organizations.)

London writers may find organizations such as Spread The Word and Apples and Snakes useful. Both of these organizations are, like the Arvon Foundation, based in the new Free Word Centre, an Arts Council funded 'Ministry of Literature' in the old *Guardian* newsroom in the centre of the City.

Congratulations! You have finished the course ... Well done. There isn't a certificate to give you, but then writing is not about certificates. Nor is it about awards, prizes, honorary degrees or smiley faces at the bottom of the page. Writing is about making the world intelligible for yourself and for others. And it's about entertainment. It's about giving your readers something they can't get anywhere else.

Ten things to do now

Write for ten minutes. Yes, right now.

1. Find a regular time in your daily schedule when you can write.
2. Join a writers' group.
3. Make sure you always have a notebook.
4. Look up the Arvon Foundation website (or order the brochure).
5. Tell everyone you know that you are a writer. Get them to take you seriously.
6. Explore writing courses at your local college or university.
7. Make contact with your nearest Arts Centre and find out about live literature events.
8. Compare your most recent piece of writing with the very first things you wrote.
9. Congratulate yourself on your progress. Have some cake, a biscuit or a beer. Buy yourself something.
10. Read a book.

Taking it further

Organizations

The Arvon Foundation
Free Word Centre
60 Farringdon Road
London
EC1R 3GA
Tel: 020 7324 2554
Website: www.arvonfoundation.org

Ty Newydd
Llanstumdwy
Cricieth
Gwynedd
LL52 0LW
Tel: 01766 522811
Email: post@tynewdd.org
Website: www.tynewydd.org

Moniack Mhor Writers' Centre
Teavarran
Kiltarlity
Inverness-shire
IV4 7HT
Tel: 01463 741 675
Email: m-mhor@arvonfoundation.org
Website: www.moniackmhor.org.uk

Gold Dust
PO Box 247
Ely CB7 9BX
Website: www.gold-dust.org.uk

Send three chapters and brief synopsis of the work in progress (novel, stories or life-writing) and your name, address and email address.

The Jerwood Foundation
22 Fitzroy Square
London
W1T 6EN
Tel: 020 7388 6287
Fax: 020 7388 6289
Email: info@jerwood.org
Website: www.jerwood.org

Arts Council England
There are nine regional offices each with a Literature Officer.
Phone for details. Tel: 0845 300 6200
Textphone: 020 7973 6564
Website: www.artscouncil.org.uk

Scottish Arts Council
12 Manor Place
Edinburgh EH3 7DD
Tel: 0131 226 6051
Website: www.scottisharts.org.uk

Arts Council of Wales
Bute Place
Cardiff CF10 5AL
Tel: 0845 8734 900
Website: www.artswales.org.uk

Arts Council of Northern Ireland
77 Malone Road
Belfast BT9 6AQ
Tel: +44 (28) 90385200
Website: www.artscouncil-ni.org

The Literary Consultancy Ltd
Free Word Centre
60 Farringdon Road
London EC1R 3GA
Tel: 020 7324 2563
Email: info@literaryconsultancy.co.uk
Website: www.literaryconsultancy.co.uk

Online distance-learning MAs

Lancaster University
http://www.lancaster.ac.uk/fass/english/postgrad/creativewriting/
creative-writing-distance.htmand

Manchester Metropolitan University
http://www2.hlss.mmu.ac.uk/english/the-manchester-writing-school

Bibliography

Where books are still available for purchase, details of the latest edition are given – sources www.amazon.com and www.bookdepository.co.uk.

If a book is no longer easily available, a search has been made on the Internet to assess second-hand availability using the search engine of Abebooks – www.abebooks.com.

Where a book has proved difficult to locate through usual retail outlets and the second-hand market, the entry has been marked 'Check with the library'.

Allen, Walter, (ed.), *Writers on Writing* (London: Phoenix House and New York: E. P. Dutton, 1948). Words about writing by some of the world's greatest writers. Both poetry and the novel are covered. Available second-hand via the Internet.

Allott, Miriam, *Novelists on the Novel* (London and Boston: Routledge and Kegan Paul, 1960). Includes quotes from Hardy, Fielding, Dickens, Zola, Trollope, Tolstoy and many others. Available second-hand via the Internet.

Archer, William, *Playmaking: A Manual of Craftmanship* (London: Chapman and Hall, 1959). Reissued 2009 by University of Michigan Library. Available via the Internet.

Armstrong, David, *How Not to Write a Novel* (London: Allison and Busby, 2003). Essential reading for anyone contemplating writing a novel. Funny, wise and true.

Ash, William, *The Way to Write Radio Drama* (reissue, London: Elm Tree Books, 1985). Radio drama techniques including plot, theme, character and dialogue. Also covers what happens when a script is accepted for broadcast.

Baker, Donna, *How to Write Stories for Magazines* (revised edition, London: Allison and Busby, 1995). Check with the library.

Bates, H. E., *The Modern Short Story* (London: Michael Joseph, 1982). A critical survey of the short story. Available second-hand via the Internet.

Bird, Carmel, *Dear Writer* (London: Virago Press, 1990). A classic guide to writing fiction. Available second-hand via the Internet.

Braine, John, *Writing a Novel* (London: Eyre Methuen), reissued as *How to Write a Novel* (London: Methuen, 1974). John Braine was both a novelist and book reviewer. This practical handbook is considered by many to be a classic guide to the art of writing a novel.

Brande, Dorothea, *Becoming a Writer* (new edition, London: Macmillan, 1996). Originally published in 1934 by Pan. Writing techniques and exercises plus how to find the 'writer's magic'.

Brewer's Theatre (London: Weidenfeld & Nicolson, 1994). A phrase and fable dictionary devoted exclusively to the theatre. Available second-hand via the Internet.

Cooke, Brian, *Writing Comedy for Television* (London: Methuen, 1983). Available second-hand via the Internet.

Cooper, Giles, *Radio Plays* (London: BBC Publications, 1982). Distinguished plays from authors such as Jeremy Sandford, C. P. Taylor and Alan Sharpe. Available second-hand via the Internet.

Corner, Helen, and Weatherly, Lee, *Write a Blockbuster And Get it Published* (London: Hodder Education, 2010). An indispensable guide for anyone who wants to write commercial fiction.

Derrick, Christopher, *Reader's Report* (London: Victor Gollancz, 1969). A publisher's reader gives the aspiring author advice on the pitfalls of submission. Available second-hand via the Internet.

Dick, Jill, *Freelance Writing for Newspapers* (3rd edition, London: A & C Black, 2003). Brought up to date to include selling to Internet publishers, and covering topics from approaching a news editor to selling rights.

Dick, Jill, *Writing for Magazines* (2nd edition, London: A & C Black, 1996). Writing and selling non-fiction to magazines, including interviewing and a section on electronic aids for the magazine writer.

Dipple, Elizabeth, *Plot* (London: Methuen, 1977). Available second-hand via the Internet.

Dorner, Jane, *The Internet: A Writer's Guide* (2nd edition, London: A & C Black, 2001). A comprehensive guide for beginners and experts alike.

Dorner, Jane, *Writing on Disk* (London: John Taylor Book Ventures, 1992). Check with the library.

Doubtfire, Dianne, *The Craft of Novel-writing* (revised edition, London: Allison and Busby, 1998).

Fairfax, John, and Moat, John, *The Way to Write* (Penguin Books, 1998). A practical guide for beginners, which explains how to evaluate and improve your work.

Forster, E. M., *Aspects of the Novel* (new edition, Penguin Books, 2000). How to see through novels, not round them. A critical revision of the text by Oliver Stallybrass has given this much-quoted title a new lease of life.

Fountain, Tim, *How to Write a Play* (London: Nick Hern Books, 2007). Clear and sensible advice on the art of playwriting.

Frankau, Pamela, *Pen to Paper* (London: Heinemann, 1961). A novelist's notebook. Available second-hand via the Internet.

Friedman, Rosemary, *The Writing Game* (London: Empiricus Books, 1999). A thoughtful and revealing exploration of creative writing.

Goldberg, Natalie, *Writing Down the Bones* (London: Shambhala Press, 1993). Encouragement and advice on many aspects of the writer's craft from an offbeat and refreshing standpoint.

Goldman, William, *Adventures in the Screen Trade* (Abacus, 1996). A personal yet practical view of screenwriting.

Griffiths, Stuart, *How Plays Are Made* (London: Heinemann, 1982). A guide to the basic principles of drama with a focus on structure.

Herbert, John, *Radio Journalism* (London: A & C Black, 1976). Gathering, editing and presenting material for broadcasting. Available second-hand via the Internet.

Hines, John, *The Way to Write Non-Fiction* (London: Elm Tree Books, 1990). Researching, writing and selling non-fiction books, market research, writing synopses, finding subject and publisher. Available second-hand via the Internet.

Hoffmann, Ann, *Research for Writers* (London: Writing Handbooks, 1999). A research guide for writers and journalists offering practical advice on organization and methods of research.

Hughes, Ted, *The Letters of Ted Hughes,* edited by Christopher Reid (London: Faber and Faber, 2007). Some terrific advice for writers as well as much else of interest to the general reader.

King, Stephen, *On Writing: A Memoir of the Craft* (London: Hodder Paperbacks, 2012)

Kitchen, Paddy, *The Way to Write Novels* (reissue, London: Elm Tree Books, 1981). A complete guide to the basic skills of good writing. Available second-hand via the Internet.

Krailing, Tessa, *How to Write for Children* (London: Allison and Busby, 1996). How to find inspiration and get new ideas on writing for children of all age groups.

Kuroff, Barbara, (ed.), *Novel and Short Story Writer's Market* (Writer's Digest Books, F&W Publications, USA, 1999). A guide to US markets, publishers, agents, contests, conferences and awards.

Legat, Michael, *The Nuts and Bolts of Writing* (London: Robert Hale, 1989). Available second-hand via the Internet.

Legat, Michael, *Plotting the Novel* (London: Robert Hale, 1992). Available second-hand via the Internet.

Legat, Michael, *The Writer's Rights* (London: Books for Writers, 1995). A comprehensive guide to the legalities and business of being a published writer.

Legat, Michael, *Writing for Pleasure and Profit* (London: Robert Hale, 1993). Comprehensive guide for beginners.

L'Engle, Madeleine, *A Circle of Quiet* (London: HarperCollins, 1998).

Long, Rob, *Set Up, Joke, Set Up, Joke* (London: Bloomsbury, 2005). A riveting – and hilarious – guide to the workings of the television industry.

Martin, Rhona, *Writing Historical Fiction* (2nd edition, London: A & C Black, 1995). Different kinds of historical fiction are covered including: the family saga, the romance, the nostalgia novel, the adventure story and the 'straight' historical.

Maurois, André, *The Art of Writing* (London: Bodley Head, and New York: Arno Press, 1960). European men of letters, including Voltaire, Tolstoy, Stendhal, Goethe and Flaubert. Available second-hand via the Internet.

Morley, David, *The Cambridge Introduction to Creative Writing* (Cambridge: Cambridge University Press Essays, 2007). Introduces students to the practice and art of creative writing.

Nivison, Kate, *How to Turn Your Holiday into Popular Fiction* (London: Allison and Busby, 1994). Check with the library.

Paice, Eric, *The Way to Write for Television* (reissued revised edition, London: Elm Tree Books, 1987). A complete guide to the basic skills of writing television drama. Available second-hand via the Internet.

Phythian, B. A., *Correct English* (revised edition, London: Hodder Education, 2010). A practical guide and reference to improve the use of English in everyday life.

Phythian, B. A., *Essential English Grammar* (revised edition, London: Hodder Education, 2010). Chapters deal with the nature and function of all principal parts of speech and sentence structure. The exercises and tests provided reinforce learning.

Priestley, J. B., *The Art of the Dramatist* (London: William Heinemann Education, 1973). The Inaugural Lecture, under the Hubert Henry Davies fund, given at the Old Vic Theatre on

30 September 1956 together with appendices and discursive notes. Available second-hand via the Internet.

Ray, R. J., and Norris, Bret, *The Weekend Novelist* (London: A & C Black, 2005). A 52-week programme to help the writer produce a finished novel.

Rodger, Ian, *Radio Drama* (London: Macmillan, 1981). Available second-hand via the Internet.

Saunders, Jean, *The Craft of Writing Romance* (London: Writers' Bookshop, 2000).

Saunders, Jean, *Writing Step by Step* (London: Allison and Busby, 1989). Check with the library.

Smethurst, William, *How to Write for Television* (London: How to Books, 2000). Information and advice on all areas of writing for TV. Revised edition includes a rewritten chapter on opportunities for new writers, plus a section on Internet help sites and workshops.

Smith, Cathy, *How to Write and Sell Travel Articles* (London: Allison and Busby, 1992). Check with the library.

Steinbeck, John, *Journal of a Novel* (Penguin Books, 2001). A collection of letters forms a day-by-day account of Steinbeck's writing of *East of Eden*, his longest and most ambitious novel.

Stillman, Frances, *The Poet's Manual* (London: Thames & Hudson, 2000). A rhyming dictionary. This volume allows writers to find easily the rhymes they need.

Strunk, William, and White, E. B., *The Elements of Style* (4th edition, Boston: Allyn and Bacon, 1999). Offers advice on improving writing skills and promoting a style marked by simplicity, orderliness and sincerity.

Trewin, Ion, *Journalism* (London: David and Charles, 1975). Available second-hand via the Internet.

Truss, Lynne, *Eats, Shoots and Leaves: The Zero Tolerance Approach to Punctuation* (London: Profile, 2007).

Vallins, G. H., *Better English* (London: Pan Books, 1955). Expands on the principles of clear writing and also deals with idiom, figure, the logical expressions of thought and the finer points of language. Available second-hand via the Internet.

Vallins, G. H., *Good English* (London: Pan Books, (1964). How to achieve a good, simple English style, whether for reports and stories or for business letters. Available second-hand via the Internet.

Wells, Gordon, *The Craft of Writing Articles* (2nd edition, London: Allison and Busby, 1996). A practical guide to writing feature articles and how to sell them.

Wells, Gordon, *How to Write Non-Fiction Books* (London: Writers' Bookshop, 1999). A step-by-step guide to writing and marketing a non-fiction book.

Wells, Gordon, *The Magazine Writer's Handbook* (London: Allison and Busby, 1985) and with McCallum, Chris, *The Magazine Writer's Handbook* (9th revised edition, London: Writers' Bookshop, 2002). For all magazine writers – detailed information on many British magazines and comments on many more.

Wells, Gordon, *Writers' Questions Answered* (London: Allison and Busby Writers' Guides, 2001). For beginners and more experienced writers alike – provides useful information addressing many of the problems that can beset writers.

Whitelaw, Stella, *How to Write and Sell a Book Proposal* (London: Writers' Bookshop, 2000). An informative and entertaining guide to writing synopses and proposals.

Wibberley, Mary, *To Writers With Love* (London: Buchan and Enright, 1993). A helpful guide to writing romance novels.

Writers' and Artists' Yearbook (London: A & C Black, 2013).

Index